FIRED
— TO —
HIRED

The Guide to Effective Job Search for the Over 40s

Paul Di Michiel

Published by Paul Di Michiel 2015

A catalogue record for this book is available from the National Library of Australia.

Book cover design and formatting services by BookCoverCafe.com

www.thecareermedic.com

First Edition 2015

ISBN:
978-0-9942983-0-0 (pbk)
978-0-9942983-1-7 (ebk)

*This book is dedicated to anyone who has ever suffered
the pain of unexpected job loss and the subsequent, often
challenging, job search that accompanies it.*

*It's for anyone who has been kept awake at night wondering how
they will find a job in a tight market, and how they will support
themselves and their family while their finances are dwindling.*

*It's for anyone who doesn't know where to start in job search in a world
that has changed since they last moved on from jobs or companies.*

*In particular, the book is aimed at jobseekers aged forty
and over who remember the days when applying for
jobs was much easier and usually more fruitful.*

*For jobseekers everywhere, I offer this book to help in
pursuit of your next job: not just any job, but one that
you will love and in which you will prosper.*

May success be yours.

CONTENTS

ACKNOWLEDGEMENTS

I have many people to thank for assisting me in writing this book. One person alone can't produce all the ideas and content, and like any author I have been heavily reliant on the people around me to complete the task.

I would like to thank Di Humphries, Chris Sutton, Kate Benchoam, Jack Hawkes, Scott Di Michiel, David Nagy, Adam Wilson, Ed Greenwood, Tim Sturt, Leain Oliver, Racquel Boyd, Jocelyn Everjuan-Baclor and Joe Powell for the time they spent talking to me, reviewing my early drafts, and offering wise and considered input. Thanks also to Paul Morrall of Paul Morrall Photography for the back cover photo.

I would also like to thank and acknowledge the many hundreds of people I have worked with in recent years. Each one has a unique story of their journey through job loss and their subsequent search. I have heard many inspiring and uplifting tales of individuals successfully surviving—and ultimately thriving—following the loss of their jobs.

I would also like to acknowledge my wonderful wife, Leearne. She is a daily inspiration to me, and others, for her selflessness and good nature. She is the person I aspire to become.

INTRODUCTION

What does it mean to be over forty? Some see it as the first real step into adulthood or maturity, while for others it's the first stage on the downward slide to old age. What about you?

Many believe there is not much to be joyful about in turning forty, maybe because it reminds us of our mortality and the belief that our lives may be half over. In many cases grandparents will have passed away, and often one or both parents have also died. We become more conscious of our position on the conveyor belt of life, which keeps moving every day, taking us closer to the end.

People often remark on how quickly time passes by, how fast children grow up, and how rapidly each week, and weekend, disappears. Sayings such as 'over the hill', 'past it', 'one foot in the grave' and 'all downhill from here' start to creep into our speech, or are mockingly shared by younger relatives and friends, to which we stoically respond, 'Don't worry, you'll understand one day.'

According to the Australian Bureau of Statistics, the median age of the Australian population is 37.3 years. In other words, half the population of twenty-three million people is younger than 37.3 years old, and half is older. This median is increasing all the time, reflective of our ageing population. If you are a male aged forty, you can expect to live to 81.3 years, and if you are a female, 84.2 years. There are 3.6 million males aged forty to sixty-four in Australia, and 3.7 million females in the same age range. That means a total of around 7.3 million people, or roughly one-third of Australia's population, are in the forty to sixty-four-year age bracket. This is the age bracket that makes up a large section of the Australian workforce.

What happens after you turn forty?

You may have put on a little more weight and are finding it harder to keep it off. Physical exercise has either taken a back seat, or you have succumbed to a slowing metabolism. You may find that your eyesight is not what it used to be, and eyeglasses are necessary for reading or long distance.

Your hearing may have declined, something that is not helped by teenage children blasting music through the house at 115 decibels or more. Your skin has become a little more wrinkled, and specks of grey may be starting to appear in your hair, which may also be disappearing. You look in the mirror and wonder what happened to that youthful, vibrant and energetic person you used to see.

The psychologist Elliot Jacques coined the phrase 'midlife crisis' to describe that moment when adults acknowledge their mortality and how little time they have left. This crisis may include discontentment or boredom with life, or with the lifestyle that has provided fulfilment for a long time. It can also extend to employment. Perhaps you are questioning your career path, and whether you want to continue on this path for the next ten, twenty or thirty years.

You may want to jump off the corporate bandwagon and find something stress free; an escape from reality and all the pressures that come with it. You may feel restless and want to do something completely different career-wise, such as buy a milk run (a running joke of mine for many years during my forties).

You may also find yourself thinking more about the meaning of life, becoming more spiritual and questioning the direction your life is taking. You may experience an increased reliance on alcohol, food or drugs; changes in sexual desire, including having affairs, often with someone younger; and decreased or even increased ambition.

By the time you reach forty, you may have spent twenty years in the workforce and have taken on larger roles with more responsibility and remuneration. You may have purchased a home, which the bank allows you to inhabit, and be steadily paying off a mortgage. You may have teenage children to feed, clothe and house. You may be reasonably well off, although you would not describe yourself as wealthy. Losing your job could threaten your financial situation immeasurably; the mortgage will still be debited from the bank account every month, utility and petrol costs will continue to spiral, and teenage children continue to empty the refrigerator, attend endless school excursions, and ask for money to go with friends to the mall.

You may feel left behind technologically, always in catch-up mode. The pace of change in this area has been incredible. Those who remember cassette tapes, and the CDs that superseded them, must now learn about memory cards and cloud computing.

Job search has also been touched by the technical revolution. There are many online job boards where you can view and apply for jobs as well as post your resume and other relevant details for potential employers.

If you haven't had to search for a job for a few years it can be hard to know where to even start within this ever-increasing and mystical technological realm.

But it's not all doom and gloom. Turning forty also has an upside. You are more mature and experienced. You have made mistakes and learned from them. You have been in relationships, possibly travelled, and worked in different organisations in different roles with, and for, different people. You may have experienced the joys and frustrations of raising children, wondering how on earth your teenagers came from your gene pool.

To a large extent you will have got things out of your system by the age of forty and discovered more about yourself. You may have achieved success, proving it's never too late to realise long-held ambitions; there's no reason to give up simply because you're a certain age.

The actor Samuel L. Jackson was a bit-part actor struggling to get by until his forties, when he landed a role in *Pulp Fiction* and achieved international recognition and fame. Henry Ford invented the model-T Ford when he was in his forties. Charles Darwin wrote his definitive book *On the Origin of Species* in later life. Ray Kroc bought and grew McDonalds into one of the world's largest and most successful fast-food chains when he was in his fifties. Arnold Schwarzenegger became governor of California at fifty-six. The actress Pamela Stephenson completed a PhD and became qualified as a psychologist at the age of forty-seven.

The point is that the main barrier to achieving your goals is probably you. Maybe you've convinced yourself that because of your age your goal is beyond your reach. A large part of success in job search is having the right mindset, motivation and practical approach to landing that next great job.

One of my clients, in our early coaching sessions, had been a little flat and unenthusiastic. He was getting over his redundancy and was feeling worn down by job search, which had included a lot of rejection. But a different person turned up to his next session; he had had some time to process things, be clearer about his career goals, and build confidence in his abilities. He was enthusiastic, active, animated and eager. He was excited about the challenge of finding his next job. While conscious of his developmental needs and potential barriers in job search, he was now more focused on what he could contribute to organisations rather than what he could not do.

Losing a job is just one of the myriad challenges we face as part of the human condition. According to the Social Readjustment Rating Scale developed by Thomas Holmes and Richard Rahe,[1] job loss is the seventh most highly rated life-stress event (with death of spouse, divorce, marital separation and a jail term the top four).

The purpose of this book is to pass on the value of my experience so you can better cope with—and meet—the challenge of job loss while moving onto your next job sooner. If you're between jobs, thinking about leaving a job, or simply have an interest in being more effective in job search, this book is for you. It is full of tips and practical guidance for anyone in job search. You will find all the information you need to navigate the challenges of modern-day job search and remove the associated fear while putting your best foot forward and confidently finding that next great job. There are no complex theories,

---

1 'The Social Readjustment Rating Scale', Thomas H. Holmes and Richard H. Rahe, *Journal of Psychosomatic Research*, volume 11, issue 2, August 1967, pages 213–218.

models or solutions, only good, practical and proven advice to give you the edge in job search.

I won't wrap you up in complicated theory, buzzwords, models or other bunkum that can be found in similar books (usually written by people who have no corporate experience, have never been in the job market, and have never experienced job loss). All the content is borne of honest, practical, effective and proven strategies, no more and no less.

My key driver is that you don't need to feel that you're going through redundancy or job search alone. You can benefit not only from my experience but others' as well; I regularly cite examples from clients I have worked with.

In chapters 1 and 2 I talk about the experience of job loss and how different elements or variables can help or hinder your job search.

In chapter 3 I offer direction if you're unsure about what your next role will be. No one can tell you what to do next, and nor is the answer likely to come to you in a flash of inspiration, but I can provide some structure to direct the thought processes and actions involved in planning for your next role.

Chapter 4 focuses on the most obvious means of job search: online job boards. This includes sites such as SEEK, probably the most visible player in the market, although not the only one. For those interested in learning more about SEEK, in the appendix you will find an interview I conducted with a senior executive of that organisation.

Chapter 5 covers cold calling and networking, additional methods of job search. Networking in particular is an important approach, given that most jobs are not advertised and employers are increasingly relying on contacts to source their employees. The belief that it's not what you know but whom you know is a key aspect of effective job search.

In chapters 6 and 7, the focus is on the role of recruiters in job search. Many people are unaware that recruiters work for the hiring company and not the job seeker. In the course of finding applicants for the hiring companies, however, they do perform a valuable service for jobseekers as well. I offer advice on selecting the best recruiters, and getting the most from them.

Chapters 8 and 9 cover the resume, the most basic collateral of job search. There are diverse opinions about resumes: how they should be written, how long they should be, what information they should contain and so on. The formula I present will markedly increase your chances of not only getting to interview but also landing that next great role.

In chapter 10 I show you how to craft a cover letter that will raise the interest of potential employers by easily and quickly matching you with the requirements of the role. I provide a template that has been positively received by hiring managers, human resources staff and recruiters.

Chapter 11 delves into the wonderful world of LinkedIn, the world's largest online professional forum. Through LinkedIn, you can develop a professional social-media presence (also known as your online brand), view advertised jobs and—possibly most importantly— connect with people beyond your immediate network or circle of contacts. Used in conjunction with networking, LinkedIn is an invaluable resource.

The penultimate stage of job search, the interview, is covered in chapters 12 to 18. Each chapter offers great practical advice, of particular value to those who haven't interviewed for a number of years. If you're worried about the job interview, these chapters are for you.

Chapter 19 covers reference checks, which usually come toward the end of the selection process. If managed well, these can be a significant differentiator in giving you the edge over other shortlisted candidates.

Chapter 20 explains what to do for the best outcome when you're offered a job.

Chapter 21 covers the transition from unemployment, or previous employment, to your next job.

Finally, chapter 22 offers direct advice from the people who act as the main gatekeepers and influencers in the hiring process: human resources professionals. The collective wisdom and practical advice of senior HR executives offers a vital look into the other side of the employment equation.

Ultimately the goal of this book is to increase your knowledge and skills in job search, thereby significantly improving your chances of being offered the job you want, whether you are in a job you don't like, or have recently lost your job due to redundancy. The strategies in this book will help you obtain the best possible outcome.

Happy reading, and I wish you every success in your job search.

PART 1

TAKING STOCK AND PLANNING FOR SUCCESS

— CHAPTER 1 —

LOSING YOUR JOB

'You cannot create experience. You must undergo it.'
—Albert Camus

If job search were easy, there wouldn't be the volume of information online, in books and the media, and in other sources that explain how to find a new role. The fact is, losing a job and having to find another can be very challenging. Unlike times gone by, it's not simply a matter of sending off a few applications and eventually landing a role. The job market is competitive, and advertised positions will produce a number of applicants, most of them qualified and well able to do the job. This means it's a great market for employers but a difficult one for those looking for that elusive next role.

After the relative security of having a job, you're now officially between jobs and marked with the label *unemployed*.

Despite losing your job through no fault of your own, this label has a negative connotation.

During my own experience of unemployment, I felt like an outsider and my confidence was affected. I could see everyone else going off to work in the morning and wondered why I was singled out to lose my job. How was I different? Why was I picked to lose my job when multitudes of other people were unaffected? I knew I was good at what I did, but despite that I found myself out of work and trying to get back into the market.

Everyone faces slightly different challenges during job loss and subsequent search, but there are some common elements. In this chapter I run through many of the obvious and not so obvious areas to be aware of and to counter during job search, beginning with a look at the bigger picture. By understanding the overall concept, you will be better equipped to develop your own methods of job search.

The economy and unemployment

It goes without saying that if businesses are not successful and growing, they are less likely to hire people and more likely to let them go. In 2014 the Australian Bureau of Statistics reported that Australia hit its highest level of recorded unemployment in twelve years (6.4 percent). This followed a surprising drop in job growth. Jobs were created, but those looking for work exceeded this growth.

The economic situation is what it is, however, and it doesn't help anyone to dwell on the statistics as an excuse for not finding work. Yes, it's difficult to find work, but not impossible. There are jobs cropping up all the time.

The information presented in this book will give you the information, strategies and tactics to win this battle and swing the odds of finding a job in your favour, even if unemployment figures are high or going up.

Time of year

In Australia you'll generally find fewer jobs in December and January. This is the summer holiday season, when people pack up the family car and head off down the motorway to the caravan park or holiday house for a few weeks of takeaway fish and chips and sunburn. Unfortunately, there always seem to be excuses at other times of the year as well to explain why companies are not hiring.

The end of the financial year is when many companies hire new staff, possibly getting in before they lose their hiring budget. Or they might have spent their budget already and are waiting for the new financial year to see if they will get additional hiring funds. Easter and other nationally celebrated holidays are other times of the year when companies stop hiring. This can be extremely frustrating for anyone desperate to find a new job.

In my opinion, the prime time for finding a job in Australia is between May and November; there are fewer public holidays, and it's a long stretch until the national annual-leave period over summer. However, there are jobs available throughout the year. If a company needs a resource, whether it's in March, September or even January, they will start recruiting for the job. This could be in an indirect way, such as posting internally for employees, or nominating people they know for the job.

The key message here is not to give up on job search completely come December, with the intention of restarting in February. By all means have a break and recharge as needed, but keep in mind that those months of downtime are an excellent time to network (see chapter 5). Not everyone has the luxury of taking off both December and January; there will still be people at work, including hiring managers.

Perceptions of age

According to a report produced by the Australian Institute of Management,[2] the Australian Bureau of Statistics and the United Nations classify workers and jobseekers as old at age forty-five, as does the Commonwealth Age Discrimination Commissioner. For those who thought old was seventy or beyond, it can be depressing to find that officially you're old at forty-five.

You can't miraculously revert to forty-five unless you have access to a time machine, a plastic surgeon, or someone to forge your birth certificate, but try to avoid building barriers for yourself by blaming your age. Very often age is thrown up as a major, self-constructed barrier to job search. I often hear people exclaim, 'I'm too old, who'd want to hire me? Employers only want younger people.'

While it's generally true that it takes those of a certain age and maturity longer to find a job, it's not an insurmountable barrier or obstacle to success. Don't give up before you've even started. Look at your age as a gift: a gift of experience; of wherewithal,

---

2 'Engaging and Retaining Older Workers', Australian Institute of Management, February 2013.

knowledge and understanding that mere pups under forty can't begin to comprehend.

People are people, however, and many hold prejudices, whether it's against age, religion, skin colour, sexual proclivity, height (or lack of it) and other anatomical features, personality, and cultural customs. These prejudices may extend to age and it's possible that you will be discounted for an available job because you remember black-and-white TV, the day Elvis died, or the Apollo 11 landing.

Despite the fact that such behaviour is unlawful, it still happens, albeit usually indirectly. One individual I spoke with had gone through a lengthy job search process, but he said there was only one occasion when age appeared to be a barrier. He had applied for a job and was invited for an interview, where he spoke with a female manager at least a decade younger than himself. During the interview she made subtle references to youth, referring to the 'young dynamic' in the company. He did not get the job, and presumably his age was at least one of the reasons behind this decision.

I say forget those people and the companies they work for; you probably don't want to work there anyway. Fortunately such people are in the minority, and there are many more enlightened and smart people and organisations that value the decades of business acumen older people bring to the workplace. They recognise the value of experience, and the skills, maturity and stability that come with it.

The best way to present yourself, regardless of age, is by the skills you bring to the table and how well you match the requirements of the job. The whole selection process is a matching exercise, so your best chance is to ensure you fit the job on offer. Believe in yourself, and don't be afraid to convey this belief as you progress through the process.

Emotions

Understandably, job loss will have an impact on your emotional state. You may feel empty because your routine and status, not to mention your income, has been taken away from you. You may understand at a deeper level that it was your *job* that was made redundant and not you, but you still wonder if you could have done something differently.

You may feel anger about the decision and how it was made. You may consider that the decision was unfair. You may feel slighted by the way you were advised. You may even have been marched off the premises without the chance to say goodbye to friends and colleagues. Many clients I meet say they don't know how their employers will cope without them.

These emotions are all perfectly normal and an accepted part of the change curve following job loss. While there is no easy way to overcome these feelings, try to stay positive. If you remain upbeat and enthusiastic despite the setbacks, you will move onto your next role sooner. You will be able to convey your skills, experiences and knowledge to all you meet with confidence, and in the right frame of mind. Redundancy affects many people, and in the modern workforce there is no stigma associated with it.

Those who hold onto their negative feelings are their own worst enemies in job search. It may sound heartless, but no employer wants to hire an overly emotional or negative person. They may empathise with your situation, but they are wondering if you will behave like that if you join them. What most employers are looking for are upbeat, positive and enthusiastic people.

So, how can you become—and stay—upbeat during the period following job loss? The next chapter will show you.

— CHAPTER 2 —

BEING BETWEEN JOBS

'All I have to do is work on transition and technique.'
—Usain Bolt

W hile you're between jobs you can help yourself immensely by keeping busy and developing a routine that allows you to block out negative thoughts and focus on more important things. Whether you use your computer calendar or sticky notes, plan out each week ahead. Not only will this keep you busy, it will ensure that you're fresh and focused and able to enjoy the moment, even in the midst of a challenging job search.

Learn from my mistakes and schedule your time effectively to stay positive. Divide your days and weeks to incorporate the following activities and you'll see the difference.

Job search. Some people say that job search is a full-time activity. I don't agree. Yes, you need to spend sufficient time looking for your next role, but it should not be at the expense of everything else. Three, four or five hours per day in quality job search is enough. The key word here is *quality*. By that I mean activity that supports your job search efforts, like engaging with others, sending off applications, networking, checking online for jobs, and meeting with capable recruiters.

Time with friends and family. When we work, a lot of things have to take second place. This often includes our spouse, partner, family and friends. Take the time during transition to indulge in things you don't normally have time for, such as picking up the children from school, having lunch with your partner, or catching up with extended family you may only see at Christmas.

Such interactions can be uplifting, and will help you recognise that there are more important things in life than work. Most people say there's nothing more important to them than family; if this includes you, this is your opportunity to prove this sentiment.

Time for yourself. Yes, you. Don't become so consumed by your search for a job that you neglect yourself, and definitely never feel guilty for indulging in a hobby or other activity during your job search. Treat it as a reward for your efforts, a means of re-energising yourself, or simply switching off. You may enjoy walking the dog, photography, crossword puzzles or watercolour painting; whatever it is, make sure it's something you have a passion for and takes your mind off the travails of job search even momentarily.

During my own eight-month job search period, at first I wasted a lot of time feeling gloomy and negative, consumed by self-defeating thoughts. Then I discovered that I could pick up my camera and tune out while looking for things to shoot, setting up the shot, or comparing angles and light. It gave me immense pleasure while taking my mind off the struggle associated with job search.

Industry trends

Think retail and the impact of online shopping. There is an increasing trend toward virtual shopping rather than physically going into a store and making a purchase over the counter. This trend will shape the way organisations are structured and staffed in the future.

Due to the high cost of producing cars in Australia, the automotive industry in this country has seen the shift of production to offshore locations. Mining is also in a structural decline, characterised by unrealistic expectations for the export of fossil fuels, such as coal to China and India. Aviation has become far more competitive, and Australian carriers are finding it increasingly difficult to compete against cashed-up Middle Eastern and Asian airlines. The price of fuel has also had a significant impact on the industry.

What is common to all of these examples is the impact on employees who lose their jobs when industries and companies scale down. If this has affected you, you may need to look at other industries as options during job search and consider any transferable skills you may have. Rather than waste time searching for a job in your old industry, you might need to investigate other industries.

You can stay aware of industry trends by keeping up with the news, both online and in print. You can also stay in the know by meeting and talking to other people; often the best and most useful information is obtained this way because it's not in the public domain or commonly known.

Location

If you live outside a major city, you're likely to find it more difficult to find work. There are more jobs in major locations (and of course more competition), and smaller towns often rely on a couple of large employers, such as mining companies, to provide jobs. If these companies go, the jobs go too.

I'm not suggesting that you move to the big city if you live in a small town, and it may not even be necessary. Be flexible. If you're prepared to look for employment in any industry, you will increase your chances of finding something. Knowing the locals and pre-existing networks can help immeasurably.

If, however, the mine in your town has closed down and you want to continue working as a miner, you have no option but to consider moving to another location. A willingness to move to places where the jobs are will always be helpful. Even if you live in a large city, time spent commuting can be significant, and how long it takes to get to and from work is something you need to consider.

It's all about compromise. If you're only prepared to work within thirty minutes of your home, you might be neglecting a large percentage of potentially available roles; however, if you're prepared to travel, you give yourself more options.

I once worked with a client who initially restricted his job search to forty-five minutes' travel time from his home (among other criteria). When he still hadn't found a job after several months, he extended this to one hour, and shortly thereafter was able to land a suitable role.

Remote, or virtual, work is another option. I once worked in an organisation where a senior product manager worked remotely from a small town in New Zealand. Head office was in North Sydney, Australia, but he was able to work effectively using email, phone calls, Skype and other technology, and needed to visit the office in person only once every few months.

When you're looking for roles, keep this option in mind as a possible alternative. If you find a role and your employer is amenable to you working from home, it could negate the impact of where you live and keep costs down, both for you and your employer, who won't need to provide office space.

Personality

If you are a shy or introverted person and find it difficult to meet other people, it could take you a little longer to find your next role. While I'm sympathetic to those with a natural reluctance to interact with strangers, this could be a challenge when it comes to performing well in interviews and addressing the hidden job market via networking (see chapter 5).

If, despite a natural shyness, you're quietly confident of your abilities, know who you are and the value and experience you offer, you stand a good chance of finding the right role. Most people you meet will genuinely want to help you, and the fact that you are a little quieter than others will not be a disadvantage if you offer solid skills and experience.

On the other hand, I would urge all extroverts to tone things down a little during job search, particularly when meeting people face-to-face. There will always be organisations and industries where being outgoing is welcome, but generally you will need to assess the situation and act accordingly. For example, you don't want to be doing all the talking during a networking meeting. Ask questions, by all means, and share personal information, but be careful not to dominate the conversation.

Gender

The unemployment rate for women is generally higher than for men, but, as with age, if a company discriminates based on gender, they reduce their available pool of candidates by half. Not a smart business, and one you probably wouldn't want to work for anyway.

On a positive note, more women are now moving into male-dominated roles such as engineering and construction, so these past barriers to entry will gradually erode to the point where gender will be a non-issue in job search.

Disappearing skills

Some professions are changing and others are disappearing. In years past, many managers had dedicated secretaries or personal assistants. Today, such employees are either shared among several managers, or managers do without and manage their own administration. Other roles that are disappearing include printers, production workers, call-centre staff, and level-1 support roles in IT, all of which are increasingly being offshored to more economical locations.

In an article published in 2013 on the website news.com.au, the writer identified Australia's disappearing jobs based on a comparison of census data between 2006 and 2011, and the representation of people in different work categories. So which white-collar jobs are disappearing?

Corporate services managers
Safety inspectors
Photographic developers and printers
Switchboard operators
Secretaries
Debt collectors
Financial dealers
Judicial and other legal professionals
Auctioneers, and stock and station agents

If you're currently in a declining profession, you may want to look at either self-development to increase your competitiveness for limited roles, or moving to a new and more stable, or growing, profession based on your transferable skills. While you're in transition, you could take a close look at your profession and the trends associated with it.

An example of a changing profession is human resources. Many typical HR roles available in the local market are for senior human-resources business partners. As part of the senior executive team, they are involved in people-related strategies designed to increase employee engagement and subsequently improve business productivity.

The old model of an HR leader with a large staff strewn throughout the business is quickly disappearing, along with transactional back-office staff and specialists in things like remuneration, recruitment and talent management. The new model has fewer in-house resources doing higher-level or strategic HR, with a greater business focus. In fact, some would argue that the people element has gone out of HR and has been replaced by a clinical, business- and numbers-driven focus. The bottom line is that HR now requires very different skill sets than was the case in the past.

Self-development

If you are willing to undertake further development to upskill, or even pursue another vocation, you give yourself a greater chance of landing the role you want. You would be taking one step back to take two forward. Perhaps you could become more familiar with Excel pivot tables, work on your time management, or complete a diploma.

Some of my previous clients have retrained in areas like social work, teaching and project management in order to pursue a new and desired role. In all of these cases there was a strong interest and desire to pursue the new career.

Going back to school may not be for everyone. It means a significant investment in terms of time, effort and cost, and acceptance that you might have to start again on the bottom rung of the ladder when entering your new profession. This can be demeaning for some, but an opportunity for others.

Self-development or retraining can open up new career options. It can take a number of forms, including going back to school, be it university, Technical and Further Education (TAFE) or other tertiary education, private study, e-learning, or learning while on the job. Whatever form it takes, for many mature workers self-development involves retraining the brain, and learning new things, possibly in a different way.

Transition, or being between jobs, can offer the opportunity, and time, to undertake projects like additional training, and a wise person will take advantage of this. It's a practical move in terms of learning something new or refreshing skills, but it can also be therapeutic to keep busy and focused on something positive, as opposed to the often-depressing thoughts experienced during job search.

— CHAPTER 3 —

DECIDING WHAT YOU WANT TO DO

'Choose a job you love, and you will never have to work a day in your life.'
—Confucius

When you are in transition, you are handed an opportunity to really think about what you want to do next. If you've been working forty, fifty, sixty, or even more hours a week, you probably haven't had time to scratch yourself, let alone plan for your next role or career. Being handed the gift of redundancy (yes, there is an upside) allows you to act on any unfulfilled career ambitions.

Many of those in corporate roles have dreams or aspirations to do something different. Maybe you have always wanted to run a cafe, work part time or change professions, but after years of scampering on the corporate hamster wheel you no longer have the inclination or opportunity. Losing your job can present you with a unique opportunity to purse those aspirations.

I once worked with a gentleman who had spent most of his career within a large organisation working in finance and IT management roles. He loved working with his team and developing them to be the best they could be. He had always considered teaching as an alternative vocation, so when his role was made redundant he decided to pursue this interest by going back to university and qualifying as a teacher. The change of careers was significant, and the outcome, and benefit, was clear. He was doing something he really wanted to do rather than something he simply fell into or that the organisation had laid out for him.

Of course, not everyone wants to do a one-eighty-degree turn away from their career, but it's good to keep in mind that redundancy and transition allows you to do this if you wish. It gives you the gift of opportunity to pursue something else. Even if you choose to stay in the same type of role, you still have a choice about the type of company you become part of, the nature of the role, and even the kind of manager you want to work for.

These benefits aside, when you're offered the opportunity to plan your next role or career it pays to approach it with the same focus and diligence you would use when deciding on a major purchase, such as a new car, or a new home.

For myself, I questioned whether or not I wanted to spend my remaining five, ten or fifteen years in human resources, a profession I no longer felt passionate about. I had lost my motivation and my heart was no longer in it. I asked myself if I wanted to continue working for, and with, those who did not have my values, even if I was paid a good salary, and enjoyed a certain degree of status and prestige. Of course, the answer was no, I did not.

Pursuing your passion

Work should be uplifting and exciting. If you're not waking up in the morning looking forward to the day ahead it's time to get out on your own terms. For many, redundancy is a blessing in disguise. I've often heard people say that they were thinking about leaving anyway and receiving a redundancy package was an unexpected, but welcome, surprise. For others, things are not so easy and more courage is needed to forge a different career path.

David was someone I had the good fortune to meet and work with. He worked in a large corporate organisation that provided financial information to traders. He enjoyed his work, and it supported his lifestyle by allowing him to travel, live comfortably and pay the bills. After eighteen years of dedicated service, and over thirty years in the workforce in total, his role was made redundant following a global restructure of the business (which also affected thousands of other individuals worldwide). David had anticipated this change, and the possibility of redundancy was both expected and welcome. Even if redundancy had not happened, he had planned to leave and pursue his passions.

Even while working in the corporate world, David had managed to use, and express, his innate creativity. He had always loved board games. He had half designed a board game, and was investigating other business options such as clothing design, poetry, and photography, even while he was working. Now he had a wonderful opportunity to plan for the future. He used his corporate skills to develop a business case for each of his ideas, and focused on developing and marketing his board game.

Living the dream as David is now doing has not come without its challenges. He freely admits there have been periods of struggle and self-doubt since he left the corporate world and focused his energies elsewhere. There will be no income for a while, and the future, while exciting, is also unknown. David and his family have had to make adjustments and give up some things to accommodate his passionate endeavours, but he remains excited by the possibilities, and sees it as an enriching stage of life.

What advice does David have for those aged over forty and experiencing job loss? 'Get in tune with what gets you excited. Treat it like a friend and nurture it. Recognise how different things can be, but don't be put off by it, or wait. You've got to have self-belief and be psychologically prepared for the change, as well as aware of your strengths that support the change. What I love drives me.'

David's story may not be the norm, but it does demonstrate that it's never too late to pursue your passions and make a one-eighty-degree turn. Do you have a passion you'd like to pursue? If so, are you ready to decide what to do next? You could start by thinking about the following points.

Your skills. Are you a great leader or negotiator? Are you a details-oriented person? Are you a strategist, writer or designer? Are you influential? What are you good at? Where do your strengths lie? You already know the answers to these questions by the results you've achieved in your career. You will also have received feedback and recognition from managers, peers, stakeholders, staff and even external parties like suppliers and vendors. Why not play to your strengths and be paid for doing so?

Your interests. What do you like to do? What sort of work do you *really* enjoy doing above all else? In your current position there's no doubt a mix of the good and not so good, so why not think about increasing the good, and reducing or removing the bad? For example, if you have an affinity for technology, perhaps you could move into a role with a greater focus on using technology, or even designing or testing technology.

Your values. What is important to you? Work-life balance? Security? Most organisations like to espouse their values on their website and on a plaque in the foyer. Do you accept this at face value, or do you know for sure that these values are practised in the organisation? Before deciding to work for a particular company, you may want to ensure that your values are aligned. If you're uncertain about what your values are, you can use a number of online tools to find out.[3] You can also ask about values during the interview (see chapter 15), or by speaking to present and past employees.

Thinking ahead

At this point you may be thinking, okay, you're telling me that if I lose my job it's an opportunity and I should examine my skills, interests and values when considering my next job. I'd love to be a lifeguard at the beach, but how is that going to pay the bills?

---

3 One good example can be found at http://leadwithgiantscoaching.com/finding-your-core-values/.

Of course, there's always a level of practicality that needs to be addressed. If you have received a redundancy, hopefully you have sufficient funds to pay the bills for a period of time. Or maybe you have a partner who can provide financially while you explore new options and perhaps even undertake additional study.

If none of these options are open to you, you might have to take a less desirable job in the meantime while allocating time to researching and finding your next ideal role. This is the tougher route, given that you will have less time to devote to job search, but it does ensure that the bills get paid. Be sure to keep an open mind during your job search, and be receptive to suggestions about other possible careers.

People may tell you that you would be great in a particular role. While well meant, comments like this are often wide of the mark, although friends and family probably do know you well and might be able to see your skills, traits, potential and abilities better than you can. So perhaps aside from mad Uncle Harry, listen to these suggestions and do the appropriate research. Once you've found a few roles that interest you, try to meet with people in those professions to learn more about possible study, or entry requirements.

It's also worthwhile looking at job advertisements. Don't worry too much about the title of the job, but pay close attention to the content or responsibilities of the role. Consider your transferable skills and how they apply to the job that has caught your eye. Keep an open mind and reflect on what you discover.

If you want to be truly happy in your next role, this will be time well spent.

— CHAPTER 4 —

ONLINE JOB SEARCH

'The truth is, we're all cyborgs with cell phones and online identities.'
—Geoff Johns, comic book writer

As you are probably aware, there are quite a few avenues for finding employment in the Australian job market, and it's worth participating in each one of them to maximise your chances of finding your next job. One such option is to investigate online job boards.

There are several online job boards available to Australian jobseekers and we will examine the key ones here. One thing they all have in common is that they are easily found on the web and accessible to anyone—although unfortunately that also means you have a lot of competition for roles listed online.

Online search is also a good way to review new or different roles you may be considering. Generally, job postings will include a job title, organisation or recruiter name, list of responsibilities, requirements of the candidate, and sometimes a salary range, all of which offer helpful information to use in job search.

SEEK (www.seek.com.au)

SEEK started in 1997, with a focus on the Australian job market, and has since expanded to include twelve countries. In any given month, SEEK advertises around 150,000 jobs, about three times more than its nearest competitor. Its primary goal is to 'connect people with careers, related learning and business opportunities'.

On SEEK you can search for jobs via the job search function by typing in keywords describing salary range, classification (for example, engineering) and location. You can also set up saved job searches, and receive regular emails relating to your chosen category or categories rather than repeating the search criteria every time. For this reason, ensure that your search details are correct before you set up your job searches.

SEEK also has a section listing jobs that pay over $150,000. This is particularly useful for more senior positions, allowing those professionals to refine their job search based on remuneration. As with other job searches on SEEK, these positions are listed by category, and include but are not limited to CEO and general management, hospitality and tourism, human resources and recruitment, and government and defence. You can further refine by keywords, location, and working hours (full or part time).

On SEEK you also have the option of setting up a profile so interested employers can find you. You complete a set template of questions advising potential employers of your qualifications, experience, and what you're looking for in your next role. You can upload your resume to your profile, set up job searches, and keep track of your applications. Only those employers who have advertised a role on SEEK can contact you, so you cannot be approached by organisations that are not offering jobs.

Another useful feature on SEEK is the advice and tips section. It includes salary survey information, advice on how to write an effective resume, guidelines for applying for government jobs, interview tips, and industry news.

SEEK is a great source for online roles. If you're not already on SEEK, it's definitely worth considering. (For those interested in a more in-depth look at SEEK, please see the appendix for an interview with Joe Powell, managing director of SEEK Education.)

Adzuna (www.adzuna.com.au)

Adzuna is a relatively new entrant into the Australian online job search scene. It has been active since 2013 and describes itself as 'a search engine for classified ads'. At the time of writing, Adzuna proudly stated that it had over 130,000 jobs listed from various job boards and employers.

When you go to the Adzuna website you're greeted by a clean home page. Start your job search by typing in a description and location for the type of job or company you're looking for. As with SEEK, you can retain saved searches and have jobs emailed to you regularly.

If you click on a particular job category, for instance 'HR and recruitment jobs', you'll be taken to a site that gives information on these types of roles, the responsibilities and skills required, appropriate qualifications, and useful links. It will show an average salary for that particular job category and list the top five employers, or recruiters, offering jobs in that category. This is useful information, especially if you want to connect with appropriate recruiters in your space (see chapter 6).

Adzuna is an aggregator site, which means it includes jobs that are listed on hundreds of other sites, including but not limited to LinkedIn, Hays, MyCareer and Gumtree, as well as a number of companies, including Telstra, National Australia Bank and Coca Cola. Adzuna's policy is to add other job feeds to their site all the time, and allow visitors to make suggestions for adding other sources of online jobs.

Adzuna also offers information streaming from their blog, with helpful topics such as 'How to impress your interviewer' and 'Resume writing tips'.

LinkedIn (www.linkedin.com)

LinkedIn is growing in importance when it comes to online job search. Recruiters love and hate LinkedIn. They love it because for a fee they can access the site and its huge database of potential candidates for open jobs. This database currently numbers 347,000,000. A recruiter can type in key terms regarding qualifications, skills and experience, plus location, industry and any other features they require, thereby generating a list of suitable candidates.

Recruiters also hate LinkedIn because more companies are now posting jobs on the site for a small fee, knowing they have direct access to a large and very broad pool of professionals, managers and senior executives. Compare this to the cost of a company engaging a recruiter and paying a percentage of the first year's remuneration; the benefits come down to simple economics. It could be argued, however, that LinkedIn job ads are more attractive to active rather than passive jobseekers, and recruiters can more ably tap into the latter.

You need to join LinkedIn, and have an account, to access jobs placed on their site. Once you're logged in, click on the jobs tab and you will be taken to a new page showing jobs that have automatically been linked to the information in your profile. For example, if your work background includes human resources, LinkedIn will naturally assume you're interested in other HR jobs. You can refine these results by filtering for location, company size and industry.

If you want to search for more specific jobs, or are interested in finding something different to what you've done before, you can search for jobs using the text box at the top of the screen. When you see the small briefcase logo at the top of the screen, type in a job title and hit enter.

You can use the fields on the left-hand side of the screen to further filter for location, industry, and keywords. Once you have a list of jobs that match your needs, you can save the search and have similar jobs emailed to you daily, weekly (or not at all). LinkedIn allows you up to ten saved searches.

Indeed (www.indeed.com.au)

Indeed is another online job site. It started up in 2004 and is less well known than SEEK or Adzuna, although a recent advertising campaign has raised its profile. It is similar to Adzuna in that when you log on you enter the details relevant to your job search in the appropriate search fields.

While the Australian site seems to pale in comparison to other online job boards, according to its website Indeed is the 'number-one job site worldwide, with over 140 million unique visitors per month'. Indeed also includes a blog and job search tips.

Jobs (www.jobs.com.au)

Owned by the Fairfax Group, Jobs claims to 'list employment opportunities across all levels from Apprentices and Graduates to CEOs and Directors'. It's a more attractive and functional-looking site than Indeed. You can type in keywords, sector and location, plus use additional search criteria like salary range, and the time period the jobs were posted.

The site also has jobseeker tools to cover any jobs you've saved, and a resume manager that allows you to attach your resume when you apply for jobs on the site.

CareerOne (www.careerone.com.au)

Part of the Newscorp stable and a sister site to Monster.com, CareerOne describes itself as a leading digital media and technology company offering innovative solutions from four key business divisions: media, tech, sourcing, and employer branding. It claims to list over 400,000 opportunities.

The website is quite busy and I found it somewhat difficult to navigate. Rather than job search options, it offers a number of text fields and a request to 'upload your resume to be found', which is a little off-putting. You have to click on the search tab at the top of the screen to start looking for posted roles on the site.

Like other sites, you can search using keywords, within categories (for example, accounting), jobs in Australia as well as overseas, full time or part time and so on. You can also do a broad search by industry, including such categories as construction, digital, education, HR and recruitment.

While you're looking at search results from Australia, you can also click on a country dropdown menu for similar jobs in other countries. This may only be useful for those who are very mobile and willing to extend their search beyond our shores.

Apply Direct (www.applydirect.com.au)

The key differentiator for Apply Direct is as the name implies: applicants apply for jobs directly with the hiring organisation or employer; no jobs on the site have been posted by recruiters or other third parties. Apply Direct claims to 'simplify the connection between the job seeker and the employer', and boasts of having a world-first, next-generation tool for job search that collects and catalogues thousands of jobs directly from each employer's website onto a single website.

Jobs are listed in all parts of Australia and across all industries. Jobs can be searched for by keywords, type (includes accounting, engineering and marketing among others), sub-type (relevant to the job type), state and city.

The website invites you to register (or 'become a member') by providing your email address and setting up a password. An immediate email will arrive to confirm your registration. You can then create up to five job-alert profiles and have relevant jobs emailed to you directly.

Another section of the site has jobseeker resources, which includes information on writing a resume, blog posts, featured job of the day, and a selection of videos featuring 'real people talking about real jobs'. There is also a section on superannuation, which seems like an odd inclusion, but it's relatively informative about issues jobseekers need to be aware of.

In a separate section on the home page Apply Direct offers access to education and training, which is where the company talks about their strategic partnership with Open Universities Australia.

All in all, not a bad concept, and it's worthwhile using Apply Direct to establish some online profiles that tap into vacancies posted directly by candidate-seeking organisations.

In addition to these sites, there are many others out there. The key point is that while no single job search activity offers a guarantee of a job, it's worth establishing your online search through all available channels. These online sources will only continue to increase in number in the future, as not only are they an economical option for employers but they are also free for jobseekers.

CHAPTER 5

OTHER METHODS OF JOB SEARCH

'It's a lack of faith that makes people afraid of meeting challenges, and I believed in myself.'
—Muhammad Ali

Apart from online job search, there are several other effective ways of finding jobs, two of which I cover in this chapter.

Cold calling

Cold calling means contacting someone you don't know, and for whom you don't have a referral or introduction. It means contacting strangers out of the blue. Rest assured I'm not advocating bombarding people you don't know with emails and phone calls, or knocking on the door of every office in your city, or walking around with a sandwich-board begging for work. There is, however, one positive aspect to cold calling: it is proactive; you are taking the initiative in job search.

After finishing university with a marketing degree, majoring in public relations, my daughter Elise had no luck finding a job in Sydney. She was contacted by a friend of a friend through Facebook with the offer of doing some piecemeal work for a company in Queensland. She made the move, and after several months the company was so impressed with her that they asked her to join them in a permanent role.

She accepted, and made the move from Sydney to the Sunshine Coast. She bought a car, leased an apartment, and acquired some furniture, but after only a few weeks she was made redundant. Understandably, this was a shattering experience. Fortunately for Elise, in her apartment block was a lovely lady who had taken Elise under her wing. This wonderful lady comforted Elise, and also encouraged her to pull herself together because, in the morning, they were going to 'hit the phones and call every marketing business on the Coast'.

Come morning, Elise started ringing around different marketing and PR firms in the area. On one call, she asked for the managing director. When asked what the call was concerning, she replied, 'It's personal.' Not the exact truth, but not a lie either. She got through to the MD and they spoke for about twenty minutes. She was invited in for an interview the following day, invited back for another interview with the MD's wife a day or so later, and shortly thereafter she was offered a job.

Very often in job search, you have to make your own luck. If Elise had not been proactive in making that call, she would never have got the job. In fact, the MD told Elise that they had wanted to recruit for the role but had been too busy. What this story demonstrates is that you can actually warm up a cold call by making a connection with someone. In Elise's case, she made a connection with the MD by showing initiative and being proactive, traits he presumably respected and wanted in his employees.

When you are cold calling, always look for a connection. That connection can come through meeting a need, membership of a LinkedIn group, or having a common ex-employer. Find a way of connecting some threads to the person you are talking with. In this way you can move from a 'cold' to a 'warm' call, with a greater chance of it leading to a job.

Here are five tips to keep in mind when making cold calls:

1. *Find companies you would like to work for; m*ake a list of companies in your industry or profession that you find attractive.

2. *Find out the names of possible contacts through* general websites, LinkedIn and other sources. (In Elise's case, she could have gone a step further and researched the managing director's name and asked for him specifically rather than by title.)

3. *Prepare and practise.* Write out a script and practise it, not to the point where you sound like a robot, but to where you sound natural and confident.

4. When you speak to the person, ask if it's a convenient time to talk. If not you can arrange an alternative date and time, but it's better if you can make your pitch when you first

speak to them. You could say that you're interested in career opportunities in their business in a certain role, or roles, and give a brief overview of who you are. This is an ideal time to use the summary from your resume (see chapter 8). Ask if you could make an appointment to meet them in person.

5. Follow up by emailing a copy of your resume, thanking them for their time and reiterating your interest in meeting, or, if you have been granted an interview, express your anticipation of the meeting.

One of the benefits of being over forty is that you probably have a little more courage borne of life experience than when you are younger, so looking for these connections and making contact shouldn't be too onerous. Even if nothing immediate comes from a cold call, you don't know what it could lead to in the future.

Networking

American author Robert Kiyosaki said, 'The richest people in the world look for and build networks, everyone else looks for work.' Networking is probably the most neglected aspect of job search, which is unfortunate as it can also be the most fruitful and productive.

If you think of the job market as an iceberg, the visible part of the iceberg consists of the jobs you find online through SEEK and other online job boards as well as those managed by recruiters and print ads (although these are rapidly disappearing in the online age). Because these jobs are visible, everyone sees them so everyone applies for them, and they often receive dozens if not hundreds of applications, poor odds for your chances of getting the role.

As a younger person I used to enjoy going to the horse races, and I can tell you that not many horses won at odds of more than five to one. In fact, I don't think I wagered on too many winners at any price. So, while you may *find* a job in the visible market, the odds are largely stacked against you.

To facilitate an effective and thorough job search, you also need to be looking in the *hidden* job market, that portion of the iceberg that sits below the waterline, where most jobs can be found. In other words, you need to be networking. These jobs fit into three categories.

Someone has just resigned. People hand in their resignations every day, for a variety of reasons. There might be things they don't like about the company, or the employer. It could be for personal reasons. They may have been asked to leave due to unsatisfactory performance. Bottom line: There's a fresh job available that has not been advertised and for which no one has applied.

HR is waiting to approve a job. Those in human resources have the important task of ensuring jobs are appropriately approved before they can be filled, and always do their best to ensure that approval is obtained as quickly as possible. I also believe in the tooth fairy.

Seriously, important aspects such as budget, head count, and current business conditions do need to be examined to ensure the job should actually be filled, and ongoing labour costs incurred. This can often take some time, since more than one signatory often has to approve the job requisition, so while the paperwork is being processed there will be a job available. If you have networked successfully, you can be at the front of the queue for that soon-to-be approved role.

There is no job. Yes, that's right, there is no job, but you could meet someone who is so impressed with your background and the value you offer that they start to speak about the possibility of you working with them. Perhaps they have an urgent business problem but don't have the resources to address it. They meet you, you have what they need, and things progress from there. In this scenario you would need to be very clear about your abilities and what you have to offer, keeping in mind how you match the requirements of any potential jobs.

A positive approach

Generally, about eighty percent of roles are not advertised and can be found in the hidden job market, yet most jobseekers spend most of their search time in the visible market where everyone else is, and where there are fewer jobs.

Accessing these hidden jobs is where networking can prove most valuable. That said, I realise that many, if not most, jobseekers are uncomfortable with the idea of networking. The redundancy process leaves many people feeling a little jaded and lacking in confidence, and the thought of going cap in hand to meet someone who has the power to hire you, or not, can be uncomfortable at best and demeaning at worst, especially for those who are over forty and have been in the job market for twenty or more years.

To make things even more uncomfortable, a typical networking meeting is filled with awkward small talk about the common acquaintance that introduced you, the weather, or the latest newsworthy event, with the elephant in the room (*Is there a job?*) lurking in the background.

At some point in the conversation you might blurt out something like, 'As you know, I'm looking for a job.' Usually there will be no job, so at this point the conversation will probably wrap up quickly with polite but quickly forgotten entreaties to stay in touch. The person you have networked with goes back to work and their day-to-day life with all its associated distractions, and you are (unfortunately) forgotten.

So, how do you overcome networking paralysis and learn to accomplish it without fear? Simple. You approach networking meetings like business meetings—*without* the sole focus being that you must get a job. I hear you thinking: What the heck, it's *not* about getting a job? Why bother then? Let me clarify.

Of course it's still about obtaining a job, but this shouldn't be the *sole* purpose of the meeting. Instead, think of it as a fact-finding mission to find out more about the company they work for. What is the hiring process? What career paths does it offer? Use the opportunity to share professional information about yourself. Show the person you are meeting a written list of companies you'd like to work for (your target companies) in order to obtain more information or insight about these companies as potential employers. Also ask them if they know anyone in these companies for potential introductions or referrals. This is far more effective than simply asking, 'Is there anyone else you think I should meet?'

Also—and this is important—ensure that you share something of value *beyond* picking up the tab for coffee. It could be something you've read online, or an article in a relevant journal, or information you've taken away from a conference you attended.

One client I worked with had attended a conference on big data, where worldwide experts were gathered. He summarised the key messages from the session into a one-page document and shared that with the busy executives he met, who often wouldn't have had the time to absorb some of the new and innovative things happening in their industry or profession. This strategy was very well received, and represented an effective and memorable takeaway from the networking meeting.

Other benefits of networking

Approach networking meetings without the pressure of finding a job, and instead focus on gathering information, making a good impression, sharing something of value, and ideally leaving with a few referrals for relevant people to meet. Those who have had experience in attending or leading business meetings, and interacting with people on different levels, can approach networking in the same way.

By not focusing on getting a job as your primary goal, the dynamics and potential outcomes will be far greater. If you were to meet one hundred people, how many do you think would actually have a job? The answer is very few. This means that most typical or poorly run networking meetings end in frustration, with people giving up after only a few attempts.

The important thing to remember is that when you network, *you* are in control. More specifically, you're in control of your brand: *you*. *You* present yourself, *you* ask questions, *you* engage with the other person, and *you* follow up. Ultimately, you control your own destiny. This is the opposite of any experience you may have with recruiters. With recruiters, you allow them to represent you and your brand in the market. You place your brand in their hands. Clearly, there is some risk in this if you select the wrong recruiter (more on recruiters in chapters 6 and 7).

Another substantial benefit of networking is that it keeps you busy. As mentioned earlier, one of the major challenges in job search is coping emotionally with being between jobs, especially if being unemployed was not of your choosing. One moment you are needed and attending meetings, completing reports, meeting potential customers and all the other activities associated with being employed, and in what feels like the next moment you're devoid of any professional activity and interactions. This abrupt transition can be soul-destroying.

When you're networking, you're keeping busy. You're setting up meetings, conducting meetings, and following up after each meeting. There's little time to feel sorry for yourself because you're engaged in productive and practical activities that not only could lead to a job, but will also increase your knowledge of professions, industries and individual companies.

One client I worked with had held quite senior roles before being made redundant from a global entertainment organisation. He spent many subsequent hours trawling through online job boards, LinkedIn, and newspapers, hoping to find his next role. This approach was safe and relatively easy, but also frustrating because he found few suitable jobs to apply for and his hit rate of getting to interview was very low. After four or five months of getting nowhere and only half-heartedly networking, he was finally inspired to get out there and meet ex-colleagues, friends and acquaintances who introduced him to others in their network, with the result that he secured a senior-executive role shortly thereafter.

Another client I worked with spent twelve months in job search, spending too much time in the safe zone of online job boards and relying on recruiters to find him a job. It was not the recruiters' role to find him a job, but rather to fill a vacancy for an organisation that was paying them for this service. Many months went by, and guess what? He got his next role via a contact in his church congregation.

One of the things I hear quite often from my clients is that they wish they had started networking sooner. So what's holding you back? Only yourself.

Start networking now. Today. Immediately.

Identify the friendly network of people you know and who you feel comfortable with, and begin with them. Boost your confidence by meeting with these folks, who in turn can refer you to others you don't know, but for whom you will be better prepared.

Don't forget that most people you meet will have been through job loss themselves at some point in their lives. Or they may have a partner, family member or friend who has gone through it. They will understand what you're going through, have empathy for your situation, and will consciously want to help you.

You may already have had people assure you, when they've discovered that you're between jobs, that they'll let you know if they see or hear anything. People who say this are usually genuine, but often they don't know how to offer specific help. Following the networking approach will give these people a real and practical way to help you.

Eight key networking points

1. Identify a number of target companies you would like to work for (at least twenty or thirty).
2. Put together a list of your friendly-network contacts and the companies they work for.
3. Set up meetings with your friendly-network contacts.
4. During these meetings, provide a brief update of your professional background, current circumstances and ask questions about their company.
5. Present your list of preferred target companies. The person reading your list might mention people they know that they could refer you to for another meeting. This will be a key outcome of the meeting: the more people you meet the greater your chances of finding the right connection that will ultimately lead to a job. This person could also give you information on organisations that could help you refine the target list.
6. Give the person you're meeting some information on a topic, subject or current innovation you have researched.
7. Send a thank-you note after the meeting and connect on LinkedIn.
8. Stay in regular contact with the people you meet. Things change very quickly in business, and regular contact means you will stay top of mind. Every six to eight weeks is perfect, and it can be a simple text, email or message through LinkedIn.

CHAPTER 6

THE ROLE OF RECRUITERS

'You need to have a collaborative hiring process.'
—Steve Jobs

Recruiters act as intermediaries in the hiring process and are engaged by companies and organisations to find employees. For example, a company may need to hire a new finance director to replace the incumbent, who has resigned. The company has options, such as direct advertising, hiring internally, or conducting their own search, but it can be more efficient and convenient to outsource the hiring process. By hiring recruiters to find the right person based on experience, skills and qualifications, the company is free to focus on their key business.

In this chapter, and the one following, I introduce you to the two main types of recruiters in the market and explain how they operate. I will cover the benefits of working with recruiters, offer job search advice from recruiters, and provide a checklist to help you select the best recruiters to partner with in your own job search.

Contingency (fee-based) recruiters

Fee-based recruiters frequently specialise in a particular space or profession, such as human resources, IT or finance. Some of the larger recruiters cover a broad array of professions, but will have specialist divisions catering to these.

The hiring company engages the recruiter and briefs them on the job responsibilities as well as the profile of the preferred applicant. The recruiter then goes into the market—via their existing database of candidates, online advertisements or referrals—to find suitable candidates. The recruiters usually do an initial screening of possible applicants to determine which are most suited to the needs of the organisation and the role on offer. This could include a phone interview and a more formal interview on their premises. They advise the HR or hiring manager in the company of the shortlisted candidates, who are then scheduled for an interview. The hiring company conducts the interviews and selects those candidates they believe are best suited for the role.

When the company has a shortlist, they may ask the recruiter to conduct reference checks on the candidates. Following this the company will either hire the person of their choice, or request additional candidates for consideration. If the former, the company pays the recruiter a percentage of the candidate's first-year remuneration. For example, the fee may be 15 percent, which, when applied to remuneration of $100,000, would result in a $15,000 fee.

Generally, recruiters also offer a guarantee to undertake another search for a suitable applicant, at no additional cost to the company, if the newly hired candidate leaves or is deemed unsuitable within a mutually agreed period of time.

Executive recruiters (also known as headhunters)

Unlike fee-based recruiters, executive recruiters tend to play at the senior end of the market ($350K plus). They also forage more in the passive job market, approaching individuals who are already employed, and may or may not have any intention of moving.

The recruiter makes contact with a potential candidate and outlines the assignment they are managing for the company they represent. They don't usually mention the company by name, but they will give a brief description; for example, they will mention that it's a multinational pharmaceutical company. They will sound out the candidate for any interest, and ideally arrange for a face-to-face meeting so they can continue to sell the opportunity.

This method of finding a suitable candidate takes time and effort, especially when the candidate pool is small. As a result, headhunters can command quite high fees, often up to fifty percent of the candidate's first-year remuneration, paid in three tranches during the recruitment cycle: at the start, after a set period of time, and upon hire.

They also offer a guarantee should the selected candidate not work out or leave within a defined period.

Benefits of working with a recruiter

If you're in the job market, it's important to find reputable and well-connected recruiters. Recruiters typically cover many diverse areas of employment, including executive placement, generalist services, and profession-specific recruitment. They are definitely one potential avenue to a new job, but the recruiter works for the paying client on consignment; in other words, the hiring company. Jobseekers will often contact recruiters believing that they will find them a job, but this is not the recruiter's brief. They have been engaged by the hiring organisation to fill a role. You, as the jobseeker, are actually getting a free service.

Beyond their ability to match you with a job, a recruiter can also be a source of information on the job market, salaries (many conduct salary surveys, which can be accessed via their websites) and other market intelligence. (I share more information about the range of services recruiters provide later in this chapter.) The good recruiters won't be precious about available jobs and will often steer you in the direction of someone they know who might be able to better assist you.

Finding a good recruiter

Unfortunately, as with most things in life, there are good and not-so-good recruiters. It's like finding a plumber. In most cases we would prefer to get a recommendation for a good plumber from people we know and trust, rather than just opening the Yellow Pages or going online. We want a plumber who will do a good job, charge a reasonable fee and not take advantage of our ignorance of all things plumbing.

It's exactly the same with recruiters. Ask people within your industry or profession for the names of recruiters they can recommend. These are the good guys. These are the recruiters who will treat you with respect and give you the attention you expect as an often-vulnerable jobseeker. They will call you after an interview, check in with you from time to time, and let you know if they have a job you may be interested in.

Unfortunately, where there is good, there is usually also bad. There are recruiters out there who are more interested in sales than people, relying less on relationships and more on a quick, high-margin financial return. Unlike the good guys, they see you, the jobseeker, as a commodity. If you have value to them (i.e. they feel they can place you easily and quickly) they will be your best friend, but if you're of no immediate value they will likely ignore you. They will talk the talk but fail to back it up with any action. They won't return phone calls or emails. If you have three interviews but don't get the job, you won't hear from them. Once you have no value, they have no interest.

The best way to avoid this type of recruiter is to ask for referrals to the good guys, and ideally arrange a face-to-face discussion so they can learn more about you and more ably represent you to potential employers. What happens if you don't have a referral? If you see a job advertised by a recruiter that you've never seen or heard of before, you're stepping into the unknown. Is this one of the good guys or one of the bad guys? Generally, it won't take you too long to find out.

Your first contact will probably be a call to enquire about the job, where you introduce yourself and ask a few questions about the role. You can make some initial judgements based on the response you receive. If you don't reach the recruiter and leave a message that is never returned, perhaps despite a follow-up email, you'll have your answer.

As with online job sources, using recruiters is a potential means to finding a job, but it should not be the only one.

One recruiter told me quite candidly that if jobseekers start out with low expectations of recruiters they wouldn't be disappointed. Unfortunately the reality is that there are very few quality recruiters out there, given that the industry is largely unregulated. Many recruiters will do the minimum: simply send out twenty resumes hoping to get one placement—and a fee. So tread warily when working with recruiters that are not known to you, or who have not been introduced via a trusted friend or colleague.

Services offered by recruiters

The 'employment dance', or interaction, has changed in recent years. In the old model, when an organisation had a vacancy they engaged a recruiter who selected several candidates they considered the best people for the job. In the new model, the candidate has greater control over the process, and is empowered to ask more questions to ascertain if the organisation and job is right for them. More importantly, the candidate can demonstrate specifically what they can do for the hiring organisation to create value or relevance.

In terms of supporting jobseekers, recruiters provide a range of services:

- Honest feedback and advice regarding job search, including feedback on whether or not they can help or if another recruiter is in a better position to do so
- Guidance on job search strategy
- Market and industry information, including trends and how this impacts hiring
- Interview practice
- Product presentation; how candidates should verbally and physically present themselves for an interview
- Help in defining what individuals are worth in the job market in terms of compensation, which is usually based on supply and demand for skills and experience
- Feedback on resumes
- Counselling of sorts, as jobseekers often struggle with things like financial issues
- Information on companies in the market, given the recruiters' direct proximity as well as market knowledge
- Follow-up to ensure that the candidate has settled into the new job and the hiring organisation is happy

Talking to a recruiter can help in job search; however, a recruiter should also set expectations about what they can offer the jobseeker. Unfortunately, few jobseekers are aware that they need to do this, and often the outcome is not encouraging.

CHAPTER 7

ENGAGING WITH RECRUITERS

'The recruiter is like a dating agency. We bring people and companies together.'
—Recruiter

This point was covered in the previous chapter but it bears repeating: if possible, tap into your networks, or canvas your friends and colleagues, for recommendations regarding reputable recruiters. Another option is to look at testimonials on LinkedIn. Recruitment is a people industry and is therefore relationship-based, where genuine trust on both sides is important.

Make contact with several recruiters and shortlist them based on your impressions. This will be easier if you have held a management position, used recruiters yourself to hire staff and have good relationships with them, but there's no reason you can't also approach them as a jobseeker. The good recruiters will either be able to help you directly or refer you to someone who can.

Maintain your relationship with selected recruiters by staying in regular contact. This will help you get on shortlists for roles more often than not because you will be top of mind.

From a more practical perspective, any selected recruiter should have a manageable workload, without too many clients. Good recruiters will often turn work away to ensure their client list is manageable and they can offer quality outcomes for all parties (versus quantity, and potentially greater earnings). This may be difficult to discern when first speaking to a recruiter, but during the first meeting or phone call you could ask how many jobs they are managing.

When you make contact with a recruiter, not only will you be assessing them but they will also be looking for certain things in you. Some points to keep in mind:

- As a jobseeker, *be willing to receive help* and agile enough to be helped. Humility is an attractive trait in jobseekers.
- Put effort into your networking and connect with people. Get word out about your circumstances and what you're looking for. Join associations and be active in them.
- *Ask yourself what you need to do to be relevant.* Find out what's happening within your industry or profession that you need to be aware of or experienced in, such as new technologies, innovations or methodologies.
- Be clear and focused in your reasons for leaving your current job or joining the organisation of your choice. What do you have to offer?

- *Present yourself professionally and energetically.* A common comment from recruiters is that only about ten percent of jobseekers present themselves appropriately for job interviews. If necessary, get professional help. That first visual impression of how you are groomed and dressed is very important (see Chapter 16).
- *Ensure you have the right attitude* when you meet with the recruiter. Treat the meeting as if you were interviewing for a hiring company.
- *Be confident, despite any rejections you may have had up to that point.* Try not to show your insecurity. Think of the meeting as a clean slate, a chance to shine. Above all, don't appear desperate.
- *Post articles on LinkedIn* to give yourself a profile as an expert in your field.

Give yourself every chance of success

If you see a job that interests you, call the recruiter and make yourself known to give yourself visibility. One recruiter told me that she might get two hundred applications for a role, but will receive only six phone calls related to the job. Beyond visibility, it also shows that you're keen. Go all out to connect. The immediacy of your call is important, as it shows that you're on the ball and using technology like smartphones or tablets to make contact.

When you do call, be vocal. Don't expect the recruiter to provide all the information without any prompting from you.

You could say that you saw the advertisement and are keen to find out more, and then give a brief overview of what you feel you can offer.

Focus on the value you believe you can bring to the role. Express an interest in the organisation, if you know the company's name and not just the position. Before you call, do some research on the business so you have something to offer that will make you stand out from the other candidates.

Never ask how much the job pays. Let the recruiter raise any discussion of remuneration to avoid appearing as though your main focus is the pay rather than the organisation or role itself.

Ensure the recruiter returns your call

One of the great frustrations of jobseekers is that they can't get hold of recruiters, or the recruiters don't return calls or respond to messages. This can be quite tough if you're in transition, and it doesn't reflect well on the recruitment industry as a whole, but don't make the mistake of assuming a recruiter will feel empathy for your personal circumstances. This may seem harsh, but it is important to see things from the other side. The fact that you've been out of work for six months and your emotional state is fragile is initially not of interest to the recruiter. They only want to know what you can offer in relation to their vacant job. It's a buyers' market, and very often recruiters are deluged with applicants for roles.

So, how can you increase the chances of the recruiter returning your call? Start by covering all the bases. Make a phone call *and* send an email to ensure greater chance of success, and you could even message the recruiter using LinkedIn.

It's also very often about how the message is left that determines if it's returned or not. Consider the recruiter and have respect for their time.

You could start by saying something like, 'Hi, Paul, my name is John Smith. I realise you're probably very busy, but I would appreciate it if you could call me back over the coming days.' Name the position you're interested in, give a few brief details about your background, supply your contact details, and offer your thanks in advance for the return call.

Meeting with the recruiter

Have a list of questions ready when you call the recruiter, just in case you are lucky enough to get through. The questions should ideally appeal to recruiter's hot button; specifically, how you as the jobseeker add value to the vacant role.

Keep the following points in mind when meeting with a recruiter:

- Appear positive even if you're feeling hard done by; negativity is not a plus. Be upbeat, well prepared, informed and have positive energy.
- If you're over forty, don't draw attention to this; it's self-defeating and will not benefit you during job search. Instead, focus on the wealth of accumulated experience you bring to the role. Emphasise your willingness to learn, and be honest about any shortfalls to demonstrate self-awareness.
- Less information in resumes and LinkedIn profiles is better than too much, so be succinct while ensuring that the information is relevant. Also be sure to adapt your resume for different jobs.
- Match your cover letter with the stated job requirements. Many recruiters will rely on your cover letter to get an initial

impression of you as a candidate, and in deciding whether to go further and read your attached resume. (See chapter 10 for more information on cover letters.)

- If you're applying for a sales role you'll find that recognition awards are of great interest and value (for example, the president's award). If you have moved sales roles every few years, address this as it could raise questions about your stability and ability to deliver sales results.
- Know your achievements and demonstrate how you would solve problems relevant to the role.
- Turn off your phone during the interview. Yes, people really do leave their phones on during interviews with recruiters—*and* answer them.
- Make sure your resume doesn't appear like patchwork; that is, a document that has been added to and updated over the years (even if it has). Critique and appropriately update the entire resume in a professional manner. Check your resume for spelling, punctuation and grammar. It's not unheard of for candidates to misspell their own names on their resumes.
- Be aware that when recruiters review resumes they pay particular attention to job location, companies, longevity in roles, job titles and career breaks.
- Do your best to attend lots of interviews, as the practice and feedback will help you become more confident.

The following checklist will help you select recruiters that suit your needs. While not exhaustive, it should give you a good idea of elements to keep in mind when asking someone to represent you and your professional brand. Apply the same diligence when selecting a recruiter that you would when engaging a lawyer to represent you in legal matters.

Item	Yes or No
Your needs are matched with their particular services; that is, they actually fill jobs you're looking for. By going on SEEK and Adzuna, you can search by recruiter to see the types of jobs they fill.	
Their LinkedIn profile contains supportive and positive recommendations and endorsements.	
Your contacts within the industry or profession speak highly of them; they have used the recruiter's services and are happy to introduce you to them as a referral.	
They have been in the industry for at least three years.	
There is sufficient information about the recruiter when you Google them to feel reassured that they know their business and are good at it.	
Your first contact with them is positive, and you feel they have your interests in mind.	
They speak knowledgeably and confidently about your industry or profession.	
They keep in regular contact with you after the first meeting.	
If they can't help you for whatever reason, they will tell you so.	

CHAPTER 8

CREATING THE PERFECT RESUME

'My experience in horticulture is well-rooted.'
—Anonymous

What exactly is a resume for? Fundamentally, it's a document in either hard or (increasingly) soft copy that you submit in response to a job advertisement that has either been placed in an online job board, or newspaper, by a recruiter or hiring organisation. Its main purpose is to get you to interview, nothing more and nothing less.

It's like baiting your hook when you go fishing. You want to be able to attract the right sort of attention, get a bite, and eventually land the big one. At the least it will allow you to get to interview, where you will have the opportunity to present yourself with impact, and potentially be offered a job.

People make many mistakes with resumes, but the main ones are: not tailoring the resume to the job that is being applied for, creating a resume that is too long and full of superfluous information, and presenting a resume that is not up to date. This last oversight often results in a mad dash to update the document, generally resulting in a poor-quality resume.

When a resume is first submitted, and assuming a human being is reviewing it, their first look at the resume is cursory. It's said that recruiters spend about six seconds reviewing a resume for the first time.

When I was interviewing, I'd spend maybe fifteen to thirty seconds. During this time, I would have in my mind the things I was looking for in terms of experience and qualifications, and be trying to find these things in the applicant's resume. If they were there, great, I'd pop the resume on the *yes* pile. If the applicant did not have the necessary requirements, it would be an easy *no*. Even if the applicant did have the necessary requirements, if they were buried in the resume and not easily found I would not spend additional time looking for what I needed and the resume would go on the *no* pile.

That sounds tough, doesn't it? In a sense it is, but usually the person reviewing resumes has a large number to get through in a short period of time. It doesn't matter to them if they reject a lot because there will probably be a good number of potential candidates to choose from.

Interviewers, be they HR personnel, hiring managers or recruiters, generally don't look at resumes during the workday. Their days are spent in meetings, calling on customers, doing reports and other such activities.

They need uninterrupted time to review resumes, which is why it's generally an activity that happens after hours. If the reviewer travels a lot, the reviewing will be done in a hotel room, over a cold club sandwich and flat diet Coke.

Knowing this, and being aware that the reviewer might be looking at the resumes when they would rather be doing more enticing activities, should give you the incentive to ensure that your resume is reader friendly. The reviewer should be able to pick it up and find what they need with minimal time and effort. A quick glance at your resume and they'll know instantly that you're a match for the role they have to fill.

Resume-reading software

> 'Unhand me, you mechanical moron.'
> —**Dr Zachary Smith**, *Lost in Space*

It's becoming increasingly common for organisations to use what is known as applicant tracking software (also known as talent recruitment systems) to receive, analyse and sort resumes submitted for roles advertised online, which, according to latest statistics, is about ninety percent of advertised roles. Some of the more common ATS providers include Bullhorn, Zoho Recruit and Taleo.

Understandably, when an organisation receives hundreds, or even thousands, of applications for roles, it can be tedious to screen, let alone read, all their resumes. ATS automates the process and replaces the human screen with a software program. In many respects this is not a bad thing as it increases the objectivity of the screening process. Plus, the software can work twenty-four hours a day, seven days a week.

ATS looks for keywords in the submitted resume in order to match the candidate to the relevant role, generally eliminating about seventy-five percent of candidates during the first cull. Keywords can even include the names of schools or universities attended, previous employers that are deemed attractive, and of course the skills and experience required by the hiring organisation.

The use of ATS is largely limited to large recruiters and businesses; however, cloud-based systems are becoming more affordable for small and medium-sized businesses. In Australia, companies using ATS include IGA, Oracle (which produces the Taleo system), Chandler McLeod, Miele, Sydney Water, Kelly Services and Mitsubishi.

If you apply for a role on a company website and are required to fill in your details as well as uploading, and copying and pasting your resume, there's a good chance you're going into an ATS. Often this process can be frustratingly long and tedious; however, if you really want the job that should give you enough incentive to get through it.

So, how can you create a resume that can be read by a robot? The best way to get an ATS to notice your resume is to anticipate the keywords or phrases the system will be trying to find for the role. This further reinforces your need to ensure that your resume is adapted to, or relevant for, the role you're interested in. If you don't tailor your resume in this way, there's a very good chance it won't be attractive to the ATS and will be among the many resumes culled as not being a good match for the role.

Brevity is best; ensure that only information relevant to the role is included. Put keywords in the summary at the top of your resume, use plain fonts, and avoid graphics and tables, both of which ATS systems can't read.

If you want to see how your resume aligns to a stated job description or advertisement, there's a great site called Jobscan (www.jobscan.co). All you need to do is copy and paste your resume in one field, the job description in the other, hit the analyse button and see the results. It will give you a percentage match rate with a skills comparison. You can use this information to further modify and update your resume so it's a better match for the advertised job.

What information should you include on your resume?

Name

Yes, put your name at the top of the resume. You don't have to include your middle name or initial unless you use this regularly, or are known as J. Robert Smith. If you come from a different culture but also use an English name interchangeably, it would be acceptable to include both at the top of the resume. Alternatively, only include the name you prefer to be addressed by, use most often, or which appears on documents such as your driver's licence.

Contact details

Add these to the top of your resume as well, but keep it simple. Include your mobile or smartphone number, and your email address.

I suggest your mobile device rather than your landline because you know you will pick it up if it rings. Many people aged forty and over have forgetful teenage sons or daughters who may neglect to pass on any messages, or, if they do, not until three days later.

Also ensure that you have a professional voicemail message on your phone for those times when you can't pick up. This is infinitely more acceptable than the theme tune to *Mission Impossible*, or you trying out your Rocky Balboa impression.

For your email address, avoid using any address that is inappropriate or not businesslike; sexymuffin@xmail.com won't help you in job search as people will infer things about you and they won't be positive. You may want to set up a new, straightforward email account on Yahoo, Outlook or Gmail that can serve as your repository for all things job search related. All email providers make it inordinately simple to set up a new email address, so make this one of your first activities in job search.

Summary

Immediately beneath your name and contact details include a brief one- or two-paragraph summary of who you are. This will describe you professionally, but it will also be an enticement or teaser for the reader to find out more about you in the body of the resume.

An effective summary will let the reader know your profession or title, the industries and companies you've worked for (especially well-known or 'name' companies), your vocational strengths, and your broader strengths as an employee or manager.

If you're an IT professional, include a list or table below the summary that outlines the software, applications and systems you are familiar with.

These are key selection criteria for IT roles, and they should be front and centre on your resume.

Here's an example of a good summary statement:

A commercially-minded human resources business partner with diverse experience across a range of industries, including IT and construction, most recently with Microsoft. Expertise in recruitment and selection of professional staff, managing talent and succession planning, and analysis of HR metrics to make effective business recommendations. Strengths include the ability to effectively manage time and set priorities; build strong business relationships with stakeholders across the organisation; and a practical and business-related approach to all tasks.

Professional history

This is the section where you outline, in reverse chronological order, the organisations you've worked for and the roles you've held. Remember, the person looking at the resume is not going to spend a lot of time examining it, so keep lists of key responsibilities down to five to seven bullet points for each role held.

When I say key, I'm referring to those responsibilities that made up most of what you did in the job. In most cases the 80/20 rule applies to our job responsibilities: we spend eighty percent of our time on twenty percent of our responsibilities. Focus only on the things that defined your role and not the minutiae.

It may be necessary to drop certain tasks and combine others, but that's fine. You really just want to give the reader a broad understanding of what you did in the role, not chapter and verse about everything you did every minute of the working day.

You also want to outline perhaps three to five key achievements per role. These items are your legacy, or key contributions, in the role. These will be the things you are most proud of and which most benefitted the organisation you worked for. They are the best of the best; the things that jump off the page and make the reader want to meet you.

I often ask my clients, 'If your ex-company erected a statue of you in the entryway to their building and listed your major achievements on the base of the statue, what would they be?'

Some good examples of strong achievement statements:

- *Introduced a new inventory management system that saved the company $10,000 per annum*
- *Trained 100 staff in 5 national locations on the new tuition-reimbursement policy within 30 days*
- *Successfully managed the offshoring of the accounts payable function to Bangalore, India, thereby reducing overall functional costs by 60%*

Identifying achievements

If you find it difficult to think about what you have achieved in previous roles, use the questions below as prompts. Did you:

- Receive any significant company recognition, such as employee of the quarter or the president's award? If so, what was it for?
- Receive a promotion?
- Introduce a new process or procedure that made a positive difference to your job or that of the department or organisation?
- Do something to save or reduce costs?

- Automate any manual or archaic processes?
- Develop new reporting that helped organisational decision-making?
- Participate in and support safety efforts in your organisation?
- Organise a major event either individually or as part of a team? What was your role?
- Lead a project team that benefitted the organisation in some way?
- Win a large account?

This is not an exhaustive list, but you get the idea. I'm a great advocate of sitting down with a pen and paper and reflecting. If you do this exercise for jobs going back five to ten years, you should be able to come up with a healthy list of achievements you can use to showcase your skills.

Currency of information

Most people who review resumes are generally more interested in your recent work history, and usually just the last five to eight years, so there's no need to add a lot of superfluous details.

Instead of listing each and every job you've held since 1975, including key responsibilities and achievements, which would mean your resume would run to many pages, find a suitable place to insert the following subheading: *Employment prior to [year]*. Under this heading, list the company name and the role you held and leave it at that. There's no need to supply individual dates because the header will cover the time period.

This approach still recognises your professional pedigree, but ensures the focus is on your recent work history, which is an evolution of your earlier career and since then you have gained experience and knowledge. Personally, I like the fact that this relevant information allows me to better understand the pedigree and background of the individual.

Here's an example:

Employment prior to 2006
ABC Holdings, accountant
Smith Engineering, assistant accountant

Education

Education includes university, college, and technical-college qualifications such as degrees, diplomas and certificates. If you are over forty, listing your high school is largely irrelevant, although I was once set right on this point. If you're fortunate enough to have attended one of the more prestigious private schools, you stand to benefit from the inevitable strong bond among the alumni of that school. This is known as 'the old school tie', and whether you left school in 1975 or 1993 is irrelevant: you're linked by a common bond that means you help other old boys or girls by offering introductions and referrals.

For most of those over forty, however, high school is so long ago it should be excluded from the resume unless there's a particularly strong achievement attached to it that may be helpful. For example, you may have been dux of the school, or scored a particularly high mark in your final year.

Professional development

This includes courses attended while employed, possibly at the instigation of your employer. They could be leadership courses for managers, courses in soft skills like presentation techniques and conflict resolution, or more practical courses on topics like safety, or computer software and systems.

You may have attended dozens of these courses over the years, but it's not necessary to include them all. Only list those that are relevant, that you can ably describe if asked. This is an important point because I've heard many interviewers over the years ask about courses listed on an applicant's resume, partly out of interest, but partly as a way of testing the applicant's memory, or perhaps even honesty.

Be prepared to say how attending the course benefited you in subsequent employment. If you can't remember the course and how you used it, remove it from your resume.

Voluntary activities

If you undertake voluntary work that may be of benefit in a job application, include it. If not, leave it off. I once worked with a gentleman who worked in the area of occupational health and safety. He had a great pedigree as an OH&S professional, but it was what he did on the weekends that turned him into an OH&S-plus candidate: in his own time he managed one hundred and twenty volunteers in a leadership capacity. This was a great selling point on his resume as it spoke of myriad skills and experience in leading others, getting things done, and contributing to his community and society in general.

Pastimes and hobbies

As with voluntary activities, only add these to your resume if they are relevant. The person reviewing your resume initially is scanning for what they want in terms of experience and qualifications, and seeing if you're a match. Something like pastimes is just noise.

In general, people don't have pastimes or hobbies that are supportive of job applications. An exception could be if someone's hobby was photography and they applied for a job with an organisation like Canon or Nikon. If they were applying for a job in these firms, the fact that they were a passionate user of the firm's photographic products could be considered relevant and of some benefit; however, that alone would not guarantee the success of the application.

Referees

All you need to say regarding referees is that you can supply them on request. Some people may claim that this is not necessary— after all, everyone has referees—but stating that references can be supplied upon request acts as an emphasised full stop to your resume, and indicates to the reader that they have reached the end of the document.

Definitely don't list your referees on your resume. This will come later in the process when the recruiter, HR person or hiring manager will ask for them. This also means that there's less space taken up with superfluous information. However if you have a referee who is well-known in your industry or profession, it may pay to include their name and contact details.

RESUME TEMPLATE

Name

Email
Mobile number
Summary

Professional experience

Job title
    Company name   Start date   Finish date
    Key responsibilities
    Achievements
Job title
    Company name   Start date   Finish date
    Key responsibilities
    Achievements
Job title
    Company name   Start date   Finish date
    Key responsibilities
    Achievements

Employment prior to [year]

Company   Title
Company   Title
Company   Title

Education

Professional development

Other skills (IT, languages, etc.)

References

Can be supplied upon request

— CHAPTER 9 —

REFINING YOUR RESUME

'I am very detail-oreinted.'
—Anonymous

You've done the hard work and created your resume, but it's not quite ready to send off to a recruiter or hiring company. Before you do that, you'll want to go through it with a fine-tooth comb to ensure that all the information is correct, that it looks professional, and there are no embarrassing errors. In this chapter I cover a list of tips and hints that can help get your resume onto the *yes* pile.

Brevity. 'Brevity is better,' is a statement I commonly make to my clients. Keep your resume to less than four pages: two to three pages is an ideal length, although this doesn't mean using an 8-point font and non-existent margins to make sure it fits into this number of pages.

Font. Gone are the days of creating resumes in uncommon and difficult to decipher fonts. Having your resume done up in an ancient gothic Roman underlined, bold, subscripted, narrow font does not help it stand out; it just means the reader will struggle to read it, become frustrated and eventually give up. It's a perceptual thing; our eyes are more used to reading commonly used fonts like Calibri, Arial and Times New Roman.

Ideally, a 12-point font is best, although 11-point text is acceptable; 10-point type is too small. You want your text to be easy to read in a dimly lit office or hotel room, and it will also be easier for you to proofread.

Don't underline the text, and go easy on the upper case as it is difficult to read and seems as though SOMEONE IS SHOUTING AT US.

Number the pages. This is an often overlooked but important detail, as it allows you and the reader to easily reference something in your resume (for example, 'On page 2 I've provided details of my professional development').

Left align headings. This means avoiding centred headings. In the Western world we read from left to right, so it makes sense to left align headers with the rest of the text on the resume. This will make it flow better and be easier to read. Having to jump to a header that is centred just makes things more difficult for the reader.

Plain is best. Further to the point about font choice and size, don't put borders on your pages. Remember, at first look the reader is only scanning your resume to see if you match their requirements.

Fancy accoutrements like borders, pink paper or logos of companies you've worked for are a waste of time and won't impress them. What *will* impress them is how well you match their needs to your achievements.

Relevance. I mentioned it earlier, but it's worth repeating: anything you include in your resume should be relevant to matching you with the job you're applying for. If there's anything in your resume that does not support your candidature for the job, it should be removed. As stated earlier, this includes irrelevant job responsibilities, hobbies, courses, and names of referees.

Legal details. You should be aware that organisations are not able to ask you about your age, sex, religion or ethnicity unless it's relevant to the job. If you want to work in an organisation that has a particular religious ethos, they are well within their rights to select from candidates who share those religious values. So unless it's a selection requirement, don't include information on your gender, age, marital status, or whether or not you have children. It's not relevant, and it can't be used to select or omit people for consideration.

Proofread. This is critically important. You should go to great lengths to ensure there are no spelling mistakes or grammatical errors in your resume. If there are, guess what the reader is going to infer? They will think you're either a terrible speller or someone who doesn't check their work, or both. This could be enough to exclude you from consideration, especially if there are a number of other well-matched applicants and many other resumes to review. Once you've checked it thoroughly yourself, ask someone you trust to also read it for spelling, grammar and the ability to be understood (in other words, does it make sense?).

In one case I'm aware of, someone who worked in finance ran a spellcheck on their resume which picked up a misspelling of the word 'fluctuation'. Unfortunately, the word-processing software duly corrected it to 'flatulence', which was perfectly spelt! True story. Always proofread your resume.

Photograph. A photograph is not required on a resume and is not common practice in Australia, although from time to time people will add them. Furthermore, there is a thought that providing a photograph identifies the individual's age, gender, and ethnicity. As mentioned earlier, none of these things can be used as selection criteria, so the current practice is to leave a photo off the resume to avoid any perception of illegal or inappropriate treatment of the applicant.

Format. Once you've completed your resume in Word or other word-processing software, save the document as a PDF (portable document format). This format generally means your resume cannot be edited without specific software, so you can be assured that what you send to the hiring organisation or recruiter is what they will see. Not everyone has the same type or version of word-processing software, and if you send it in its original format you risk your beautiful resume being corrupted by the recipient's version of your software. While this will not be your fault, it won't convey the right sort of professional image you're hoping for.

Recruiters. Sometimes recruiters will either want you to format your resume in a particular fashion, or take the information in your resume and adapt it to their format. This makes sense, especially if they send the hiring organisation several resumes. A consistent format makes the documents easier to read and compare. If this is the case, you will have to accommodate their wishes, even if it means you can't use your own format.

From time to time you may also find that recruiters will tell you to include additional information, or show information in a particular order. Again, you should comply on the basis that the recruiter will be representing you to the hiring organisation and you want them to do this as effectively as possible.

This chapter has covered a lot of ground in relation to the presentation of your resume, which is the most fundamental and obvious part of job search. It is a document you will use constantly; not only will you send it to hiring organisations and recruiters, but you will also pass it to networking contacts and post it on job boards like SEEK.

The information will help you to develop your resume or update an existing one, but you may choose to have a career coach or resume expert provide you with guidance. Be careful, however, as some people purport to produce job-winning resumes that are actually nothing more than nicely formatted documents with little or no substance, and which contradict many of the suggestions provided in this chapter. Some of these so-called resume writers will charge over four hundred dollars to write your resume after having only a brief conversation with you about your background beforehand.

Be very careful if you do select someone to work on your resume. I recently saw one of these resumes and quickly noticed quite a few spelling and grammatical errors, not something you would expect when forking out a lot of money.

I recently worked with a gentleman who had not updated his resume in over twenty years. He wanted to bring the document up to date because he felt his current role was at risk and, as an insurance policy, he wanted to proactively start applying for other roles. I sat with him for ninety minutes, asking him questions and clarifying things he said. Together we developed a great resume that summarised him professionally, identified key job responsibilities and high-impact achievements going back twelve years, as well as adding relevant professional development courses undertaken. His resume was simple and contained high-quality content that gave him every chance of getting to interviews.

In summary, make sure your resume is tailored to the requirements of the job you're applying for; include key words and phrases to help ATS find you; ensure that you include specific information in your resume with a particular focus on achievements that indicate how well you have performed in your previous jobs; and follow the resume tips provided to markedly increase your chances of getting to an interview and one step closer to your next job.

CHAPTER 10

WRITING A COVER LETTER

'Enclosed is a ruff draft of my resume.'
—Anonymous cover-letter writer

A cover letter is still generally required when applying for jobs. Many people combine their cover letter with their resume when submitting online so there's only one attachment with their application rather than two, which could be more time-consuming for the recipient to handle.

Often the individual who has crafted a cover letter will spend hours, if not days, putting together a wonderfully detailed and convincing editorial as to why they are the best person for the job. This typical text-heavy tome will include reference to the job applied for, reasons why they are a good match, and how they would love to discuss the opportunity further in an interview.

Not only is an application like this voluminous, but most recipients won't even read it. Large chunks of text are not appealing, and given that most readers will only devote fifteen to thirty seconds to reviewing the resume, they'll spend even less time, if any, on the cover letter.

Ideally, a cover letter should be no longer than one page. It should include an opening paragraph stating your interest in the role and explaining why you believe you are a strong match. List the selection requirements, and match them with your relevant experience, knowledge and qualifications. It doesn't matter if you present this information in table format, bullet points or aligned paragraphs. What does matter is that your qualifications for the role match the ones being asked for.

What if there are a lot of essential requirements in the job advert? Suddenly your cover letter has gone over a page. In this situation, I suggest two things. Firstly, surmise from the advert what you believe are the key criteria. Secondly, call the hiring manager, recruiter or HR person and ask them what the critical requirements are for the candidate they are seeking. You can then match these against your background in the cover letter.

Below this, include a brief paragraph that outlines your availability. If you have recently been made redundant, you're letting them know that not only do you match what they need, but you can also start straightaway. Before starting a new job most people have to give notice, which can be anything from one week to twelve weeks or even more, but if you're between jobs your availability for an immediate start is a distinct advantage.

If you have worked in the corporate environment, you know how painfully slow it can be to get approval for new or replacement jobs. Not only are people scrutinising the role and questioning why a replacement is needed, but requisitions to hire also get lost, people go on holiday, or they delay approving for their own reasons, generally related to saving money. On the back end of this, if the candidate (you) can start sooner, that can be very attractive.

Here is a cover-letter template that you can use in your job search. When using this letter with clients, I have only ever heard good feedback; usually my clients have been told that it was easy to see how they fit the requirements of the job.

COVER LETTER TEMPLATE

Name of recruiter

Company name

Address or email address

Dear [name of recruiter]

My name is [name] and I would like to formally apply for the [position] recently advertised in [publication/website] on [date]. I am a strong match for the role based on:

Job responsibilities	My background

My role at [last company] was recently made redundant and I am able to start immediately [or provide earliest possible date available]. I look forward to hearing from you and can be available as required for an interview.

Yours sincerely

[Name]
[Email address]
[Mobile phone number]

— CHAPTER 11 —

SETTING UP A LINKEDIN PROFILE

'Technology is a useful servant but a dangerous master.'
—Christian Lous Lange, Norwegian Nobel Peace Prize recipient

I referred to LinkedIn earlier in relation to online job search; in this chapter I will go into more detail about how you can use LinkedIn more broadly during transition and beyond.

LinkedIn was founded in 2003 and, according to its website, now has approximately 350,000,000 users. That's right, 350 million. In Australia, there are about six million members and growing. LinkedIn is part of the social-media phenomenon, and while you may have some reluctance participating in social media I strongly urge you to get on board with LinkedIn and set up an effective profile.

Before you do this, however, you might like to check out your online profile. Enter your name into Google and see what comes up. If you are already on LinkedIn, your profile should be the first thing that appears unless you're involved in other activities outside of your professional life.

Increasingly, employers and recruiters are going online to check out potential applicants ahead of an interview. In my role as a career coach, I always make a point of searching for people on LinkedIn before I meet them. This allows me to learn a little more about their background, while also giving me an impression of them professionally.

In this chapter we'll spend some time going over what I consider to be the key elements of creating a powerful LinkedIn profile. There are three advantages to being on LinkedIn.

1. **Professional image**. Your LinkedIn profile page becomes your 'landing page' in social media. When someone searches for you in Google or LinkedIn, the first thing they will see is your profile. The question is, do you want this profile to leave a good impression of you or a poor one? This is a rhetorical question; of course you want to give the visitor a good and strong impression.

   When they first see your profile, perhaps prior to meeting you for a coffee or even an interview, they'll see your photo and find out from your headline who you are professionally, the jobs you've held and companies you've worked for, and recommendations of your work and endorsements of your skills.

   Your profile is your electronic calling card (or 'a business card on steroids', as I've also heard it described).

2. **Networking**. Back in the dim dark past before the internet, we put the details of the people we knew in the alphabetical section of our diaries and kept a large stack of business cards. Or we had fantastic devices like the Rolodex that was full of addresses and phone numbers of friends and people we met through business. Our visibility was limited to our own personal contacts.

   One of the most powerful functions of LinkedIn is that it gives you visibility to an expanded network, which is a crucial part of business today, and allows you to connect to people beyond your own contacts; in other words, the contacts of your contacts. It also allows you to see the people you know who work in, or have worked in, particular companies. If you don't know someone directly, there's a chance you could know someone indirectly, which will facilitate further introductions or referrals.

   In essence, LinkedIn gives broader visibility to your extended network during job search, and, as we saw earlier, most jobs are not advertised but instead filled by people speaking with and engaging with others.

3. **Jobs**. As we saw earlier, LinkedIn is one of the best online job sites around, attracting interest from both companies and recruiters. If you're not on LinkedIn, you won't have access to these posted roles and therefore have one less potential channel into the job market.

Creating a profile

Hopefully I've convinced you that being on LinkedIn is of immense benefit, and you're ready to create a LinkedIn profile. So, what makes a great profile? It's a combination of many things, and it doesn't take a lot of time or effort to put together. It constantly surprises and concerns me to see half-completed or half-hearted attempts at LinkedIn profiles. This can only have negative inferences that can so easily be avoided with a little time and effort.

I suggest that as a starting point you complete your resume and use this as the base for your LinkedIn profile. Remember that your resume and LinkedIn profile are two separate communication tools that you use in job search. You generally send or email copies of your resume directly to companies, recruiters or networking contacts, but with LinkedIn, anyone with a computer and an internet connection can find you and scrutinise your profile. That could potentially be hundreds of millions of people, so you really want to be sure it's in good shape.

The following steps will show you how to set up an effective LinkedIn profile.

1. **Content:** To register, go to www.linkedin.com, enter your email address and create a password. Once you've done this, LinkedIn will guide you through the setup and you'll have a basic profile you can start populating immediately.

2. **Photo:** It's been said that recruiters are six or seven times more likely to look at a LinkedIn profile if there's a photo, and if they do look at the profile, they will spend about twenty percent of the time looking at the picture. Preferably this

will be a professional photograph, but a viable option is to ask a friend or family member who has a DSLR camera (to ensure quality) to take your photo. It should be a sharp, well-lit head-and-shoulders shot. Dress as though you're going to an interview. Looking into the camera works best, and a smile will endear you to the viewer more than a sombre look.

Once you have a good photo, it should be cropped square to fit the space on the LinkedIn site. It should be no larger than four megabytes; files of around 300 kilobytes are perfect.

3. **Headline:** LinkedIn allows 120 characters under your name to describe who you are professionally. When people are already in a job, they tend to include the name of the company and their job title. If they are between jobs, however, understandably they don't have this option. It's better to describe who you are rather than use a mundane job title like 'finance analyst' or 'marketing manager'.

I would also shy away from stating that you are 'seeking next opportunity' in your headline. Instead, include something in your summary that speaks to your current between-jobs status, and specify the type of job you are after (see summary below). The rest of your profile should then address your suitability for these roles.

Some good examples of effective headlines:
- Experienced financial analyst with diverse industry experience
- Commercially astute human resources business partner
- Sales-driven general manager within the pharmaceutical sector

At a glance, any of these headings will convey the gist of who you are. Even for those working in organisations, there's a trend away from titles to phrases that either describe the job undertaken, or what it's set up to do. It may take some time to get your headline right, but it will be worth it.

4. **Connections:** How many connections should you have? LinkedIn is about connecting with others, not just for job search but also for business in general, including business development and information sharing. When you connect with others, you build relationship bridges that can serve you well in all these arenas. It really is true: it's not what you know but whom you know that matters.

   If you look for companies as part of your job search, you'll be able to see how you're connected to those organisations. Both first-degree connections (people you know directly) and second-degree connections (people your first-degree connections know) serve as conduits into organisations you'd like to work for. (Third-degree connections are another step removed and unfortunately there is limited opportunity to contact them unless you convert second-degree connections into first-degree connections.)

   Using Google as an example, type 'Google' into the search field at the top of the screen and hit *enter*. This will bring up Google's company page. On the right-hand side of the screen it will tell you how you're connected, indicating any first- or second-degree contacts. In the absence of any first-degree connections, you can then click on second-degree connections to see how you're connected to them via a mutual connection.

Whether or not you can be introduced to people in identified companies will rely on the strength of the relationship on both sides: your side and that of your mutual contact to the individual within the company. For example, if the mutual contact is an ex-colleague and family friend of the person you'd like to meet, great. But if your contact is someone you met briefly at a conference five years ago, this will not be very useful because they won't know enough about you.

I suggest that you aim for at least one hundred connections; even more would be better. This may seem insurmountable when you first start on LinkedIn, but the number will quickly add up if you include ex-colleagues, friends, family, next-door neighbours and anyone else who could be beneficial to you in business and job search.

The beauty of LinkedIn is that it suggests connections to people you may know based on the information in your profile. For example, if you worked in a company for a certain period of time, it will present other individuals who worked in that same company over the same period.

You can also search for individuals by typing their name in the field at the top of the screen. If it's a common name like John Smith, you may be presented with forty thousand individuals sharing that moniker. You can refine your search by adding the country, current or past company, and any other criteria you think of (some of which is only accessible if you have a paid LinkedIn account).

5. **Contact details:** You may have the best LinkedIn profile on the planet, but if people can't contact you it's all for

nothing. On that basis, ensure that your contact details are spread across your profile. You can include your email address, phone number, Twitter website links, and any other information you feel comfortable with. Remember, whatever you put on your profile (depending on your settings) can be accessed by anyone with an internet connection. If you don't mind who calls you, include your phone number. If you'd rather limit contact to email, only include your email. You get the idea.

On a separate point, there appears to be a glitch in LinkedIn where occasionally the contact information below the profile picture does not appear. To counter this, LinkedIn has included another section further down the profile where you can add additional information such as relevant contact details.

Some people add contact details in the summary section at the top of the profile. This is not a bad idea, especially if you've kept this section brief. You can also add a brief paragraph outlining the type of role you're looking for as well as your contact details in the summary (see point 7 following).

6. **Public profile URL:** A URL (uniform resource locator) is essentially a website's address (for example, www.google.com). Your LinkedIn profile is basically a website within a website and has its own unique URL. This will give second- and third-degree connections access to your public profile, and first-degree connections access to your more complete profile.

When you first join LinkedIn you will receive an auto-generated URL link that sits beneath your profile picture. Being auto-generated, it will not be tailored and will include additional details that make it quite lengthy and a little untidy (for example, au.linked.com/pub/Michiel-di-paul/45/417129/en).

When in edit mode on your profile, click on the small icon to the right of this URL and it will take you to a new page that contains your public profile URL. Again, click on the pencil icon to the right of this link and type in your name. If you hit save and it sticks, great, you have a new public profile URL. If your name has already been taken, LinkedIn will offer you available alternatives or you can continue with your own versions until the system accepts one.

Not only will your public URL look cleaner on your profile, but you can copy the link and include it on your email signature, business cards, Twitter account or anywhere else you would like to give people access to your LinkedIn public profile.

7. **Summary:** This should be a short, concise overview of who you are, professionally presented in the first person (*I am an experienced financial analyst*), where you have obtained your experience in terms of industries and companies (*I have worked in transportation, IT and pharmaceutical industries, most recently for XYZ company*). List your vocational strengths or expertise (*C++ programming; talent management and succession planning*), and your strengths as an employee or leader (*My strengths include the ability to manage both local and remote teams*).

In the same way that the summary in your resume should encourage people to keep reading, your LinkedIn summary should encourage them to scroll down a few additional screens to learn more about you.

8. **Experience:** This is where you include brief information about your work experience (resist the impulse to copy and paste information from your resume). I recommend a brief paragraph to describe your key responsibilities, and perhaps one or two major achievements that you would like to highlight.

     Avoid adding any confidential information that could be detrimental to your previous company if shared publically. It's often safer to use percentages rather than actual figures as well (*I increased revenues of the product by 10%*).

     Keep information regarding more recent roles to eight or ten lines. For roles going back eight or more years, just include the company name and logo, position held, and dates. If you're over forty, people will reasonably expect that you've been in the job market for a while. Don't feel compelled to include every job going back to the Neolithic era. Use your judgement. Include what you feel is relevant and what you want represented in the broader market.

9. **Recommendations:** LinkedIn gives you the ability to ask for mini-references, or recommendations, which you can attach to the relevant company and job role on your profile. Your connections could provide you with a recommendation from your profile page, but this rarely happens. More commonly, you would request a recommendation from them.

     As with general references, it's perfectly acceptable to provide a level of coaching to those you request recommendations from. If you want the person who is recommending you to mention your work with regard to a particular project, achievement or skill, ask them.

To ask for recommendations, go to the small picture icon at the top right-hand corner of your screen, click on it and select 'Privacy and settings'. The system may prompt you to enter your password again prior to going into the settings page.

Towards the bottom of the settings page you will see 'Manage your recommendations'. This will take you to another screen, where you have the option of receiving, giving, or asking for recommendations. Click on 'Ask for recommendations' and LinkedIn will provide an email template you can send to a connection for a recommendation. (You can also get to this screen via a dropdown list to the right of 'View profile as' on your profile screen.)

You can't ask for a recommendation if you're not connected to someone, but if you are, fill out the template, being attentive to personalising your message, and send it to your connection. Your connection will see the recommendation request in their LinkedIn inbox, complete it and send it back.

Rest easy; the recommendation won't be visible in your profile unless you allow it. Should the recommendation come back with a few spelling errors or omissions, you can go back to your recommender and ask them to edit it and return it. When you're happy with it, you can publish it on your profile or leave it off at your discretion.

Recommendations are a fantastic supplement to your LinkedIn profile. Even though you may write an excellent profile to project your professional image, recommendations carry additional weight because they are professional endorsements from those you have worked with or for, or have supervised.

If you don't have any recommendations currently on your profile, I suggest obtaining at least one or two for your roles over the last five to ten years. These will be the jobs most people scan as they scroll through your profile. Furthermore, only two recommendations per job show up, so having more than two doesn't add extra value as far as the casual viewer is concerned.

10. **Skills and endorsements:** Similar to recommendations, those you are connected to can endorse the skills you've captured on your profile. The first step here is to ensure you've included all your relevant skills. You're allowed up to fifty skills, so make sure you include all of them, whether they are technical, operational, soft, or leadership. These skills will help others, including recruiters, find you when they search using keywords.

Ensure that keywords and phrases such as 'talent management' or 'Javascript' appear at least 3-4 times throughout your profile in addition to the skills and endorsements section. This increases your chances of being found by recruiters and larger organisations that scout LinkedIn looking for suitable candidates.

Once your skills are listed on your profile, your connections can independently endorse you by clicking a plus sign against each skill when they view your profile. LinkedIn will occasionally ask if you want to endorse connections for certain skills when you first log into your home page. After a while, endorsements of your skills by your connections will paint a picture of the skills you possess.

Unfortunately, this section of your LinkedIn profile can be diluted by well meaning but ignorant connections endorsing you for skills they are not in a position to comment on. For example, a gentleman my mother dated several years ago knew I worked in HR. When I connected with him on LinkedIn recently, he started to endorse me for a number of HR skills. While this was well meant, the endorsements were not valid because his knowledge of me was very limited. Fortunately, LinkedIn allows you to remove such endorsements.

11. **Additional info:** You can include information about your interests and personal details, adding as much or as little as you wish. If you include your date of birth (you can exclude year), your connections will be advised when it's your birthday and may send you birthday wishes. If you don't want to be reminded of the rapid passing of time beyond your fortieth year, just leave this blank.

    I've chosen to include photography in my interests, and if I click on this highlighted link in my profile it will show other LinkedIn users with the same interest. I could, if I wished, use this as a networking tool to find other photographers, both in my first-degree and broader connections.

12. **Groups:** During periods of transition, there is a risk that you may lose your currency of knowledge within your profession or industry. While you could use other sources to stay in the know (seminars, industry journals), LinkedIn groups gather together like-minded individuals to share information, raise questions, and discuss topics of interest in a virtual context.

    For example, as a photographer I could go to 'Search for people, companies, jobs and more', select 'Groups' from the dropdown menu and enter 'Photography Australia'. I would be presented with a number of groups, including commercial photography and Australian photography. I could then click on each to discern if they were suitable for me based on the description of the group, and whether any of my connections were also members of that group.

Being a group member allows you to see discussions in progress, and whether group members are discussing or debating topics of interest. You can also initiate discussions as part of your group membership. Being a group member is a good way of staying up to date with developments in your field, and it also allows you to build a virtual presence among others in your profession or industry.

LinkedIn has both locked and open groups. Locked groups have a small padlock icon beneath the group title, which you click to join. The group facilitator will allow membership or not, based on your profile. This functionality is largely to keep out the spammers, who tend to target group sites.

When you join a group, you will receive emails about all activity in that group. If you don't wish to be bombarded by dozens of emails every day, simply unsubscribe at the footer of the email. You can also click on the 'i' at the top of the group page to access the settings, where you can change the type and frequency of the communications you receive.

13. **Companies:** You can also choose to follow a number of companies. LinkedIn's default settings will include your current or most recent company (which you entered when you first registered for LinkedIn), but you can also select other

companies to follow. Select 'Companies' from the dropdown menu and type in the name of the company. Once in the company page you will see information about the company as well as how many people follow the company, including any of your first- and second-degree connections, and information about how many employees of that company are on LinkedIn.

In relation to first- and second-degree connections in the company, this function is a real benefit when it comes to networking. If you want to work for a certain company and discover an old colleague now works there, you could contact them and see if they are free for a coffee to discuss entry requirements for working in that company.

If you don't have a first-degree connection, you could use your second-degree connections to get introductions that could serve as a conduit to your next role. This is one of the greatest benefits of LinkedIn in job search.

If you're interested in a particular company as a potential employer, follow it. There are no barriers to entry; simply click on 'Follow' and you will start to receive updates on that company on your LinkedIn home page. The company logo will appear on your profile, indicating you are following them.

14. **News, influencers and schools:** You can also follow news feeds on topics of interest (careers), key people of influence in diverse areas, from authors to business gurus (Bill Gates, Richard Branson) to world leaders. I have a second-degree connection to Barack Obama, the president of the United States, and I could potentially join his over one million followers on LinkedIn.

There is more information than you will ever need on LinkedIn, so some dexterity is required to ensure you don't overload yourself with information. I suggest you take a considered approach to whom and what you follow, and ensure that whatever you get is valuable. If not, the useful information you receive may get lost in the noise.

15. **Honours and awards:** Don't be shy to crow about these. If you've received any significant forms of recognition or reward in your professional life, or during your studies, include them here. I wouldn't drill down to things like an email from a happy customer, but corporate recognition as employee of the quarter, or the president's award, would be valuable inclusions.

    LinkedIn also allows you to move the order of various sections. For example, my profile on LinkedIn (http://au.linkedin.com/in/pauldimichiel) has my honours and awards right under my summary. Go into 'Edit profile' and you'll see double-headed arrows in the upper-right corner of each section. Drop and drag sections in the order you wish them to appear. In my case, I believed that my honours and awards were better placed on the first screen visitors to my profile see rather than buried deeper in my profile, which is the default for this section.

16. **Courses:** Here you can include relevant areas of professional development. You can also attach such development to particular jobs, which means they will hang under that job description on your profile as well as in a summary section further down.

Once your profile is set up, LinkedIn will prompt you to make it more complete (often quite irritatingly so). This can occur when you first log in, or by going to 'Add a section to your profile'; this function offers a dropdown list of sections you can choose to add to your profile (for example; volunteering, languages, publications).

A gauge will appear to the right of your profile showing a ranking for profile completeness. While it's satisfying to get an all-star ranking, if you complete the steps outlined above you will have a profile that serves you well on all three fronts mentioned earlier: professional image to the market, facilitation of networking, and job search.

LinkedIn is becoming an increasingly important location for online jobs. What's more, it's free, and it's intuitive to use regardless of your level of online competence or age. Social media is the future, and it will only continue to be more dominant in job search, both for organisations looking to fill jobs and candidates on the job market. If you don't climb onboard you may miss a significant conduit to your next role. You may be over forty, but you should never be too old to embrace this sort of technology.

How do recruiters use LinkedIn?

Larger recruiters and organisations use what's called 'LinkedIn recruiter' to search for both passive and active jobseekers. In essence, they pay LinkedIn to use the site as a database, which gives them access to everyone on LinkedIn along with the ability to communicate with them via LinkedIn's mail service.

You may have received an email in your LinkedIn inbox about a job from a recruiter, or a talent acquisition specialist with a large organisation, and wondered how they stumbled upon your profile.

Well, they didn't stumble; they searched within LinkedIn using relevant search terms (*Sydney, financial analyst, pharmaceuticals*) and found you that way.

All the recruiters I spoke with in the course of writing this book told me they use LinkedIn to obtain information about candidates, and very often to post jobs. The immediacy of the information on LinkedIn means it can be accessed easily using mobile devices, tablets, laptops or desktops.

In summary, you need a complete and effective profile on LinkedIn as part of your job search strategy. It not only conveys who you are professionally when someone views your profile, but more practically facilitates networking by not only using your first-degree contacts (people you know), but also by leveraging second-degree contacts (people your first-degree contacts know) to provide introductions to people in targeted organisations.

One last tip: if you need to make mass updates to your LinkedIn profile after reading this chapter, make sure you turn off notifications to your network. If you don't do this, your network will be bombarded by each and every change you make to your profile (*Paul has a new photo, Paul has a new headline, Paul has added experience*). You get the idea.

To turn off updates, go to your profile screen and on the right-hand side you will see 'Notify your network?' Make sure you turn this to 'No, do not publish an update to my network about my profile changes'. Make your mass changes, wait forty-eight hours and turn it back to 'Yes'. Then when connections visit your profile they will see your wonderfully complete and professional profile.

— PART 2 —

THE INTERVIEW

CHAPTER 12

THE INTERVIEW #1
A CLOSER LOOK

'I had a job interview at an insurance company once and the lady said,
"Where do you see yourself in five years?" and I said, "Celebrating
the fifth year anniversary of you asking me this question."'
—Mitch Hedberg, comedian

Apart from the resume, the interview is the most obvious element of job search and also the one that strikes the most fear into people's hearts. Why is this? Many people don't like to be the centre of attention, talk themselves up, or be put in a situation where they don't know the answer to a question. All valid concerns, but none of which are insurmountable in job search. I suggest countering each of these concerns as follows.

Being the centre of attention. In an interview, you are part of a two-way discussion. Yes, the interviewer wants to find out about you and your suitability for a role, but you also want to know if the organisation, role and manager suit you. Interviews are similar to networking meetings. Think of them as business meetings, where it's as much about you finding out about them as it is them assessing you.

Talking yourself up. I often comment that there's no place for modesty in interviews, but at the same time it's not the time to be brash or presumptuous either, which I can guarantee will put off most interviewers. Instead, convey your skills, experience and knowledge in a confident fashion. You are, in effect, selling yourself to the interviewer, so put aside those notions of being humble and meek. Be confident in who you are and how well you match the requirements of the job.

Not knowing the answer to a question. While this may happen, if you're well prepared you'll be able to anticipate and answer most questions. If you're not prepared, then clearly you will struggle. I've seen this all too often over the years, when someone's preparation for an interview was apparently putting on the new suit, gelling their hair, and reading their resume on the bus while journeying to the interview.

Types of interviews

There are several types of interviews, all of which are looking at the same things: whether the candidate is a good match for the job; and if they will fit in with the manager, the team and the organisational culture.

The process can be objective in terms of structured behavioural questions, but it can also suffer from large doses of subjectivity and gut feel on the behalf of the interviewers. Hence, interviewing is often termed an inexact science because it's difficult to predict with absolute certainly if someone will be a good fit and ultimately successful in the new role and organisation. As a result, many organisations conduct a number of interviews, reference checks, assessments, presentations, case studies and other methods to increase the odds of a better match.

Interviews can take a number of forms along a continuum. On one end is the panel interview plus reference checks, assessments, and meetings with the team and senior management. On the other end of the continuum is the informal coffee meeting, where the individual has some information about you from their contact and wants to meet you to see if the chemistry or cultural fit is right. Regardless of the type of interview you attend, preparation is the key ingredient.

The main types of interview format:

1. **One-on-one interview:** This format is still relatively common, especially if you're meeting a recruiter or perhaps even a hiring manager you would be working for.

2. **Panel interview:** This is where you are interviewed simultaneously by a number of people. It could be two people or as many as seven, as I once experienced. The benefits of the panel interview for the company are that all the relevant stakeholders can interview the candidate at the same time and be in receipt of the same information. They can then collectively discuss the suitability of candidates before making the decision to hire or not. Assuming it can be arranged around people's schedules, the panel interview is time-

effective compared to a number of one-on-one interviews conducted over a period of weeks or months.

If you attend a panel interview, be sure to give equal eye contact to all members of the panel, even the person who asks very few or no questions; this may just be the individual who has been instructed to make up the numbers and doesn't really want to be there. Eye contact creates a good connection with the panel interviewers and doesn't give Mr or Ms Grumpy any recourse to say, 'I didn't trust him. He didn't look at me the entire interview.'

3. **Skype, Google Chat, or other virtual interview:** These are generally one-on-one encounters where the interviewer and candidate are in different locations. They are convenient to conduct and save time, but don't have the same personal connection that comes from a face-to-face meetings. Also, technology doesn't always cooperate; it can be subject to gremlins, like delayed audio or frozen screens, which can be irritating for everyone.

The benefit of a Skype interview is that you can have your resume and other documents in front of you and out of sight of the interviewer. You can glance at your materials occasionally but still maintain eye contact via the camera lens.

Always make sure that you're appropriately dressed for a Skype interview. Don't assume that because it's virtual, it's somehow different. You're attending a formal interview so dress the part. Don't do the newsreader trick either, unless you're confident you won't have to get up during the interview. I heard about one situation where the person had to get up to retrieve something during the interview, giving the interviewer a nice view of their pyjama pants.

Also make sure you let family, flatmates and any others you live with know that you're having a Skype interview and don't want to be disturbed. Place a sticky note on the door to avoid interruptions. Make sure pets are out of the room and can't be heard if they start howling at the moon.

My son Edward had the unfortunate experience of leaving a door open during a Skype interview for his first job. The family cat, Jigsaw, decided to pay him a friendly visit and jumped on the table to say hello. Edward saw Jigsaw coming in his peripheral vision and swept her off the table with a well-aimed right arm, but she caught the edge and was left dangling while Edward continued to answer questions and maintain a professional demeanour.

4. **Screening interview**: These are usually conducted over the phone and the main purpose is to confirm that you have the key requirements before the organisation calls you in for an interview. The caller takes away an impression of you during this verbal exchange, including how confidently you answered the questions, your tone of voice and your enthusiasm.

5. **Group interview**: Not so common, but I hear of them occasionally. In this case, the interviewer or interviewers will call in anywhere from three to eight candidates and throw questions at them randomly. Sometimes the candidates answer the same question, and at other times they respond to a mix of questions.

Clearly, this is a competitive situation designed to see who stands out. For the interviewers it's an effective way of culling the candidates to a manageable number, but it can be challenging for the candidates. Not only do you have to answer the questions, but you must also deal with the dynamic of trying to stand out from the crowd.

This type of interview is generally one-sided, in that you will not usually be given the opportunity to ask questions of your own. One client I worked with described a group interview with a not-for-profit organisation as extremely uncomfortable because everyone was trying to outdo each other; the interviewers acted like 'autocratic ringmasters'. It was not a good experience, and my client felt she had no opportunity to shine or present her capabilities.

6. **Case studies**: In this situation, which generally forms part of an interview process rather than being used as a stand-alone tool, you will have a business scenario to work on. You may be given certain facts and information, mimicking a typical situation faced in the workplace, and asked to devise a solution. The organisation reviews your proposal, looking closely at your methodology. This approach can be a practical means of assessing an interviewee's suitability.

7. **Presentations**: Should you make the shortlist, you may be asked to present on a particular topic to the hiring manager and other key stakeholders in the business, most of whom will have a vested interest in the outcome of the selection process. You may have fifteen, thirty minutes or longer to deliver your presentation, which you would have prepared in the preceding days or weeks.

Similar to case studies, presentations give the hiring organisation the opportunity to see you perform in a real-life scenario, not only in terms of how you plan and think out a presentation, but also your physical delivery and response to questions. It goes without saying that full preparation is imperative.

How many interviews will you have to attend?

The short answer is, it depends. You could be invited to attend one interview and be offered a job shortly thereafter, or you might have to attend an ever-increasing number depending on the organisation and the individuals they want you to meet as part of the decision-making process.

I worked with one client who attended ten—yes, ten—interviews for a regional sales role in a large information-technology organisation. He met with a recruiter, a talent-acquisition specialist, the hiring manager, a senior HR person, the regional head, and various other individuals locally, regionally and within the corporate head office in the United States. As he went through the process, the number of other candidates dropped off until there were just two candidates left. Unfortunately for my client, he was the second choice for the role, which he found hard to take given the time he had invested.

A typical interview process would see a first interview, and possibly a second or third. Very senior roles may go beyond this, but most people can bank on two or three interviews followed by reference checks and assessments prior to an offer being made.

It's fair to say that if a selection process is too longwinded it may be indicative of an organisation's decision-making culture. Do they equivocate over other decisions for equally long periods? If this style of management does not suit you, it may be a point to consider when weighing up a job offer.

Questions to ask prior to the interview

When you receive the call to attend an interview, you should ask two questions: Who will be interviewing me? What should I do to prepare for the interview?

If the caller doesn't tell you who will be interviewing you, you should ask, as knowing the person's role in the organisation will help you prepare for the interview. For example, you could use LinkedIn to look at the interviewer's profile and see if any of your first-degree connections know them. You could then ask those connections about the interviewer's leadership style, their likes and dislikes, their interview techniques, and the method by which they select people.

Some people don't want to be seen looking at someone else's LinkedIn profile, particularly if that person is going to interview them in the near future. But if I were the interviewer, my reaction would be that this person is preparing appropriately for the interview, which I would see as a positive thing. If you feel uncomfortable with this, however, there is an option within LinkedIn for making your profile anonymous when viewing another individual's profile.

Asking what you can do to prepare for the interview is another way of obtaining valuable information. The person you ask may blow you off and not give you anything of value, or they could give you a snippet worthy of additional preparation time. For example, they could tell you they are interested in your experience at another organisation and want to explore that in more detail, or they could describe the role and let you know they will be asking about your experience in that area.

Choose your time and prepare

If you're given the choice of an interview slot, I suggest you take the earliest available. Why? If four or five interviews are lined up for a particular day, the interviewers will be most fresh, excited and anticipating a good day *before* the interviewing process begins. If you've done the necessary preparation and do a great interview, you will become the benchmark against which all the other candidates are compared.

Additionally, after two or three average or uninspiring interviews, the interviewers are starting to think about lunch, going home or that fascinating pattern on the office carpet.

Preparation is critical, and I believe it may be the most important part of the interview process. It really is true that if you fail to prepare you should prepare to fail. You generally only get one shot in an interview. All too often I've heard people say they'll 'wing it' at their upcoming interview, and wing it they do—right out the door of the interview room, never to return.

An important point: most interviewers are not well prepared themselves, and sometimes not prepared at *all* for the interview. This means that you can be better prepared than they are. It gives you the upperhand and should also calm your nerves.

CHAPTER 13

THE INTERVIEW #2 RESEARCH

'Research is creating new knowledge.'
—Neil Armstrong, astronaut

Important tip: *never* run late for an interview. I have had candidates arrive for interviews anywhere from a few minutes to fifteen minutes late and not even offer an apology. Running late is the mortal sin of the interviewing world and guarantees you'll be cast down to the fiery furnace of rejected-candidate hell. The interviewer will assume that if you can't get to the interview on time you'll never get to team meetings on time, or submit your reports on time.

I've even heard of some interviewers simply refusing to see candidates who arrive late for an interview without explanation, believing that timeliness is a critical aspect of the job and their organisation, and that by being late for interview the candidate demonstrated that they didn't value the company's time or their own. Tough, but I hope that most interviewees who have had this experience learnt their lesson.

In saying this, I recently met a candidate who arrived one hour late for his interview. Miraculously, the interviewer waited for him to arrive (which, by this stage, was six-thirty pm) and interviewed him for three hours. Given the lateness of the hour, the interviewee offered to drive the interviewer home afterwards. He was offered the job a few weeks later.

I once saw a cartoon that showed some particularly eager interviewees camped outside the organisation overnight before their interview. You don't need to go this far, but make sure you do know where you're going, and be sure to arrive around ten to fifteen minutes before your interview.

If you know you're going to be late, despite your best efforts to arrive on time or even early, call ahead and explain that you're running late, and by how much. If it's only five or ten minutes, most interviewers will accommodate this; if you're going to be more than fifteen minutes late you may forfeit your opportunity to interview for the job because there will almost certainly be other interviews scheduled for that day. Bottom line: don't ruin your chances before you even arrive.

Additional points to focus on when preparing for an interview:

1. **Know your resume inside and out**. Your resume is like a script that the interviewer will use to ask you about past experiences. Logically they'll want to know more about some

of your achievements and how they pertain to the role they are looking to fill; however, they could also ask about some innocuous piece of information hidden on page three or four of your resume.

The overly inquisitive interviewer will try and catch you out by asking you to tell them more about the training course you did, or ask what you took away from the course that you applied in your subsequent experience. They might seem like innocent questions, but they are designed to see how well, or otherwise, you prepared for the interview. If you don't answer well, it could count against you when they make their decision.

2. **Be prepared for difficult questions**. Not surprisingly, you will be asked to respond to questions on the 'essential requirements of the selected candidate' as per the job advertisement or description. Over the years I've interviewed people (usually those who wing it) who made it obvious by their responses to the questions that they had failed to read the job advert properly. If the ad asks for experience in dealing with diverse stakeholders across the business, you should be prepared with several specific SAR stories that illustrate your experience and success in this arena (see chapter 15 for information on SAR stories).

It's not rocket science; it's common sense, but very often in interviews common sense gets thrown out the window. By doing the simple things well, you can put yourself ahead of the other candidates and closer to a job offer.

3. **Research the company**. One question you can generally expect in an interview is, 'What do you know about our company?'

If you answer this question with a trite, ill-prepared response you may as well get up, walk out of the interview room and go home. There is no reason not to know at least six to eight key points about the business you are interviewing for.

Years ago, before the internet, information was difficult to find and we all had to rely on the local library or management association, but now we have instantaneous access to all the information we'll ever need.

One online tool you may find useful when researching companies is Glassdoor (www.glassdoor.com.au). This website allows you to look inside an organisation by typing the name and location into the search box. You will be presented with general information about the company, including website address, number of employees, revenues and competitors. You will also find reviews of the company by both past and present employees, citing pros, cons and advice to management.

One of the criticisms of Glassdoor is that employee—and particularly ex-employee—reviews of the company can have a negative slant, on the basis that an aggrieved employee or ex-employee can vent their spleen online in the safe cocoon of anonymity. The original American Glassdoor website has far more data than the Australian website, and is therefore more useful. (There were only fifty reviews of Qantas, one of Australia's largest companies, on the Australian website at the time of writing.)

Another tip is to tailor the information you research about a company to the job you are applying for. For example, if you're in finance, focus more on that side of the organisation.

If you're in HR, gather details about interesting people or HR facts. The more prepared you are, the more solid will be the perception by the hiring organisation that you will work to a similar standard if hired.

4. **Research the interviewers**. As mentioned earlier, this is another instance where LinkedIn comes in handy. Before your interview, go to LinkedIn and look at who is interviewing you. Find out how you're connected to them. If there's a second-degree connection (i.e. someone you know who is connected to the interviewer) you could contact the person you know, tell them about your interview and ask for details about the interviewer. What is their leadership style? Has the person you know ever been interviewed by them?

   This strategy is dependent on a strong connection, but used judiciously it could give you great information to use to your advantage in the upcoming interview. You need to use any advantage you can during the interview phase and this is one obvious, and generally underutilised, area that could help you.

5. **Prepare questions to ask**. You will usually be given the opportunity to ask questions, either during the interview or more commonly towards the end. If it does come at the end you won't have a lot of time, so stick to the questions that will be critical in *your* decision-making process should a job offer come your way.

   Unfortunately, interviewees often make a number of mistakes when asked if they have any questions. These include:

   • Mistake #1: The interviewee says, 'No, I think you've answered all my questions.' To me, this response is almost like saying, 'I haven't really thought about the job or the company and so I haven't prepared any questions.'

- Mistake #2: Just for the sake of asking a question, and to avoid mistake #1, the interviewee blurts out something like, 'Is the job based here?' The interviewer will think: Of *course* the job is based here, you dodo. Didn't you read the job ad?
- Mistake #3: The interviewee focuses on minor, unimportant issues, or asks a question like: 'Is there any weekend work involved?'

A far better way of using this opportunity to interview the manager and the company is to ask about things that are important to you in considering the job and the company. This could include career advancement, professional development, empowerment, and the leadership style of the hiring manager.

Ask if the position you're interviewing for is a new or replacement role. If the former, why was the role created? If the latter, why did the last incumbent leave? Was there anything they did or didn't do that the organisation was either happy or unhappy about? If you're stepping into an existing role, it's always good to know how the previous incumbent performed.

One of my previous clients wanted to find employment in a social environment where people worked hard, but also had opportunities to socialise. She was interested in whether or not companies had a social club, or a social culture. As this was important to her, I urged her to ask about it when she attended interviews. This became a key piece of information for her in considering offers.

6. **Know where the interview will be held**. If you haven't been there before, don't wait until the day to familiarise yourself with the location. You want to avoid stress and arrive at the interview relaxed and ready to give of your best. Look up the address on Google Maps. Better still, if you're going by car drive to the location the weekend before your interview. That way you can drive around, see where to park, confirm the location of the company, and generally just get your bearings if what would otherwise be an unfamiliar environment.

7. **Know what to wear and check the dress requirements**. Generally it's better to be overdressed than underdressed (think about sitting in an interview in a polo shirt and chino pants with interviewers who are wearing suits). To be sure, check for dress standards with the person who will be interviewing you, or the recruiter who teed up the interview. Interviewers judge on first impressions, and your physical appearance on the day of the interview is all part of the selection process (see chapter 16).

CHAPTER 14

THE INTERVIEW #3 STANDARD QUESTIONS AND RESPONSES

'I cannot think of any strengths, only weaknesses.'
—Anonymous

Most managers have very busy schedules and often move from one important meeting to the next, usually with only a few minutes in between. Many use this valuable, albeit transitory, time to scan resumes. Note that I said 'scan' and not 'read'. They will only have picked up snippets about you before they enter the interview room, and typically they will revert to off-the-cuff-type questions.

There are many potential questions, but the list below represents questions that I have seen asked on many occasions by hiring managers because they require little or no preparation. Plan for these questions as part of your preparation routine. Beneath each question I have given guidelines for possible answers. Tailor your own answers to fit your particular circumstances.

What can you tell me about yourself? Use a spoken version of your summary as outlined in the chapter on resumes.

Why did you leave/want to leave your last job? Be brief, matter of fact, objective and non-emotional in answering this question. For example: 'Unfortunately, as a result of offshoring of the engineering function my role and others' roles were made redundant.'

If you're resigning, be honest but not controversial. If you're leaving due to a terrible boss, don't say your boss is an obnoxious so-and-so and you need to get away. Instead, focus on the pull factors drawing you to the job you're applying for, which should be paramount anyway in terms of your interest in the role. This may include things like interesting work, career progression, the industry or anything else that attracts you.

What are your strengths and weaknesses? Think of your strengths as your selling points as they pertain to the requirements of the role. You don't want to be too obvious and simply parrot that your strengths match (ironically) exactly the requirements of the job, but you do want to demonstrate that your strengths match what the company is looking for. They could include working as part of a team, presenting to large groups, or analysing data. In all cases you should be able to validate such strengths by providing specific examples, the rationale being that if you have successfully demonstrated such skills in the past, you can do so in the future.

Coming up with weaknesses is a challenging question for most interviewees. If you say you don't have any weaknesses, it's clearly untrue; we all have developmental needs. Over the years I've encountered overconfident and poorly prepared candidates who have said exactly that, and in the process dismissed themselves from consideration. We often fear that we will say something too significant, which will discount us from consideration. The safest bet is to use a real developmental need (note that I'm changing the word 'weakness' to something with fewer negative connotations) and then outline how you have overcome or are working on that developmental need.

You could say something like, 'Probably my biggest developmental need has been around time management. I've improved my time management skills by diligently keeping a task list and calendar of events as well as checking in with my manager each morning to ensure that I'm aligned with their priorities for the day.'

The key thing here is to show self-awareness around the developmental need, as well as actions taken to either improve or overcome the perceived weakness. You also want to cite at least one example to illustrate your improvement in this area, as most interviewers won't just rely on a general response about how you have improved.

The weakness question is not particularly useful; however, preparing an appropriate response will help you avoid the panicked feeling of not knowing how to answer the question.

What do you see yourself doing in two/five/ten years' time? The subtext of this question is to gauge your ambition—or lack of ambition—and whether or not you have a plan in place for your professional career. You should answer the question honestly; if you don't have aspirations to be a CEO you should feel comfortable saying so.

Alternatively, if you do harbour such goals, make sure you verbalise this as well. For those who are happy with their position on the corporate ladder, one response could be, 'Assuming I'm able to learn and contribute in my next role, I'd like to think that in the coming years I could take on the role with increased responsibilities and scope.'

What didn't you like about your last job/boss/company? The key thing to avoid here is being negative, cynical or sarcastic in any way. Your manager may have acted like a power-hungry narcissist, but you can never say that in an interview. Instead, you could say something like, 'Even though my boss and I occasionally had different views, I learned a lot from them.' I've often heard from people who say that they learned the most from their worst managers—generally what *not* to do.

I once worked for a manager who delighted in demeaning and belittling her staff when she felt things were not done correctly. As a result, I've never demeaned or belittled anyone who has worked for me, knowing the damage this behaviour can cause.

Why do you want this job? This question offers a great opportunity to explain how your background fits the requirements of the job, and to demonstrate your knowledge of the company and how attractive is the prospect of working there. Avoid telling the interviewer that you are out of work and need a job, so when you saw their advertisement you applied immediately. This response will guarantee you'll *remain* out of work.

Why are you interested in working for us? This is similar to the previous question. Determine the pull factors you find attractive in the organisation and role, relate those to your professional background, and explain how you can contribute.

What are you most proud of in terms of accomplishments? If you've prepared your resume as outlined earlier, you'll have a number of achievements to select from. We all have a couple of achievements that sit above others in terms of our positive recollections: use those that are relevant to the role in question.

What would you aim to accomplish in the first thirty/sixty/ninety days on the job? This is important, as it indicates how quickly you would get up to speed in your new role. You don't have to overcomplicate this; you could mention understanding the key priorities of the business, your boss, and other key stakeholders you would be working with and for. Present your plan for developing solid business relationships with all relevant stakeholders, including peers, staff and even outside suppliers or vendors.

You also want to look for quick wins: things you can accomplish early on to gain credibility and a foothold in a new organisation, where, understandably, people will evaluate you as the new person and sit back to see how and what you are going to contribute. The information you researched on the company and the job means you should have a basic framework for what you would do early in your tenure to validate the organisation's decision to hire you.

Why should we hire you? Don't say, 'Because I'm the best candidate, duh.' (Yes, people do say this.) Instead, outline how you fulfil the requirements of the job and would approach solving the challenges faced by the business. You are being hired to do a job, whether it's to analyse results, sell widgets, or develop people; whatever the organisation is willing to pay for. Ask yourself what you bring to the table. How do your skills and experiences meet the organisation's needs and add value? How can you solve the problems they face?

What are you earning/did you earn in your last job? While the inclination is to add a few thousand dollars onto your pay to get a bigger increase when joining, your best bet is to be honest. In the (unlikely) event you are found out, the employer will understandably be questioning the honesty of all your other responses and, worst-case scenario, could even terminate your employment.

What are your salary expectations? Always give an indication of what your salary expectations are, even if only asked about your last salary. Why? Because what you were earning at your last company may not be the best indicator of your worth.

Fundamentally, the market—or what most companies pay for a role in a particular industry—determines what you are worth. If you were working for a company that paid low in the salary range and you ask for what you were earning there, you would be doing yourself a disservice. Instead, while in transition you have the opportunity to review job adverts, visit recruiters, study online salary surveys (generally produced by recruiters), network and interview with other organisations, and as a result have the information you need to determine your true worth.

You could respond to this question by saying something like, 'Given that I've been in job search mode for several weeks/months now, I've had the opportunity to research the market via job ads, recruiters, salary surveys and other means, and on that basis I'm looking for a salary of approximately [*fill in the blank*], exclusive of superannuation.'

— CHAPTER 15 —

THE INTERVIEW #4 INTERVIEW TECHNIQUE

'The harder I practice, the luckier I get.'
—Gary Player, golfer

Years ago, interviews were relatively unsophisticated and focused on general confirmations and questions such as, 'Have you dealt with customers before?' Interviewers may have been pleased to know you had worked in customer service as indicative of your skills in that area, or that if you had managed people you were an effective manager. There may also have been hypothetical questions asking what you would do if faced with a certain situation, such as dealing with a poorly performing employee.

Interview technique has changed since those days. The process has become more detailed and extensive. Interviewers no longer accept information on resumes at face value, and instead probe into what candidates have done to validate their skills.

Most interviewers will ask what is known as behavioural interview questions, which are usually prefaced by, 'Can you tell me about a time when ...' or 'Give me an example of ...' or 'Have you faced a situation where ...'

Each of these questions is designed to elicit a specific response that illustrates desired skills. The interviewer might ask, 'Can you tell me about a time you successfully managed a difficult customer?' You could give an example of how you did this in a previous role, the premise being that if you've managed this successfully in the past you will be able to replicate this going forward. In essence, past behaviours are the best predictors of future success, hence the term 'behavioural interviewing'.

When responding to behavioural interviewing questions, there is an effective strategy to structure your response for maximum impact: situation, actions and result (SAR).

Situation

Describe what was going on at the time. Set the scene. What challenges or obstacles did you face? Using our difficult-customer example, you could say something like, 'As a customer-service representative I took calls from customers on a variety of issues. About six months ago, I received a call from one of our biggest customers, who was very unhappy about his most recent order not being correctly fulfilled. He was very aggressive on the phone and wanted his issue fixed immediately.'

Actions

What did you do to deal with the situation? What was your response to the incident and the obstacles? You could say, 'Despite the customer's attitude, I allowed him to speak and I listened carefully to confirm my understanding of his concerns. I promised to follow up immediately by speaking to my supervisor and the team involved in sending out his order, which I did. I found that his order was not completed accurately and discovered the cause. I then called the customer to explain what had happened and said I had organised a delivery of his outstanding item in the next three hours. I also explained how the error had occurred and what I'd done to correct future orders.'

Result

In explaining the outcome of your actions, you could say, 'The customer was very happy with the outcome and apologised for being so upset earlier. His wife had been hospitalised and he was feeling very stressed. While I was on the phone with him, he placed another larger order and continued to trade regularly with us.'

I often describe the 'R' for 'result' in SAR as the big finish to your story as it demonstrates the business benefit of your actions. Make sure that you present the outcome—the result of your efforts—in organisational terms as best you can. In our example, saying the customer was 'happy' only tells half the story. The real impact—the business impact—is that the customer continued to trade with the organisation.

The benefits of the SAR approach

This approach allows you to demonstrate a range of skills. Using our example, the interviewee conveyed skills in listening, following up, prioritisation, decision-making, collaborating and client liaison. When an interviewer is looking for certain skills in the vacant job, SAR stories will convey factual, real-life examples of those. Furthermore, if customer-service skills are a key requirement of the job, the interviewer may ask for two or three examples to ensure you have what it takes to perform a similar role in their organisation. One example may not be sufficient to demonstrate that you have the key skills required.

As you have gathered, SAR is very effective in answering behavioural questions. It allows you to convey your response in a well-structured, logical and easy manner. It also ensures that you can be time-efficient in your answers.

Interviewees who are unprepared tend to waffle, be long-winded and fragmented in their response to behavioural questions as they retrieve—and attempt to piece together—details from their subconscious brain. Both the delivery and the content are nowhere near as strong as with the SAR approach.

Be mindful that the person who is interviewing you does not know your company, you or the situation you are describing, so give enough information to ensure understanding. This requires some judgement on your behalf. Don't give too much superfluous detail. If the interviewer wants to know more, they will ask. For example, they could say, 'You mentioned that you met with the team involved in the order. Given that they had made an error, how did you approach this?'

141

I recommend that you have SAR stories to expand on achievements listed in your resume as well as against the requirements of the job. You don't need to write out the SAR story as part of your preparation; simply note a few bullet points that bring key points to mind and enshrine them in an effective structure. One SAR story can demonstrate many different skills. Your action now is to prepare and practise your SAR stories as you step into the job market.

CHAPTER 16

THE INTERVIEW #5 PRESENTATION

'Appearances are a glimpse of the unseen.'
—Aeschylus, ancient Greek writer

Sir Edwin Hardy Amies, founder of the Hardy Amies fashion label, once said, 'A man should look as if he had bought his clothes with intelligence, put them on with care, and then forgotten all about them.' How you present yourself at an interview is extremely important, as it may be the first impression the organisation has of you. As the saying goes, 'You never get a second chance to make a good first impression.'

Dressing up makes us feel special and lifts our mood. It's appropriate that we feel confident heading into an interview because it keeps us upbeat and ready on the back of excellent preparation.

As soon as the interviewer sees you they will draw inferences based on your appearance. You want to be perceived as professional, enthusiastic and someone who has made an effort. By doing this, you're also showing respect for the people you're meeting.

Turning up to an interview inappropriately or shabbily dressed almost guarantees that the interview won't go well, as people will be wondering just how badly you want the job. Your appearance would indicate that you're not really that interested. It's all about inference, so ensure any inferences are positive ones.

It's also smart to be aware of seasonal dress. During Australia's very hot summers, it's unreasonable to expect someone to attend an interview wearing a suit. You'll not only arrive in a sweaty lather, but you'll also be uncomfortable during the course of the interview. In saying this, most interviewers will invite you to get comfortable and take off your jacket.

You should also dress for the industry or company you are interviewing for. It's no surprise that working in a legal practice is formal, with suits and ties mandatory. Legal work often involves dealing with clients, and dressing this way also conveys signals like *successful*, *smart* and *trustworthy*.

For high-tech jobs, where many workers sit behind a computer all day with little, if any, interaction with external clients or visitors, more casual dress is the norm, with T-shirts and ripped jeans common.

If you are asked to an interview on a Friday, it may be the organisation's casual, or dress-down, day. You could check with the recruiter or HR person ahead of time, but it would be prudent to turn up smartly dressed regardless.

Additional tips for men

Men, make sure you're cleanshaven when you turn up for your interview. If you must have stubble, ensure it's neat and well trimmed. Comb or brush your hair, and avoid excessive gel and other flammable substances on your cranium. Make sure your shoes are clean and polished, and worn heels or soles are repaired. Ensure that your shirt is ironed, and that your clothes have been dried properly and don't smell musty.

Don't make the mistake of wearing someone else's suit for the interview. If necessary, buy a new one; it will be worth the investment. If you plan to wear your own suit but haven't worn it for several years, try it on in advance to make sure it fits, and clean those stains from your cousin's wedding three years ago. Avoid the temptation to wear a green or purple suit, orange trousers, or any other garish colours unless you're going for a creative job where you know such outfits are the norm. The same applies to flashy jewellery, nose rings or dog collars.

Wear a tasteful tie (avoid pink elephants or beer bottles) in a colour that matches your suit or trousers; make sure the knot is neat, and your top shirt button is done up. Wear matching socks, ideally in a dark colour, that go at least halfway up your calf. It's never a good look for a hairy leg to poke out during a leg-crossing manoeuvre.

Use deodorant or antiperspirant; you will get sweaty before and during the interview. You will be memorable, but for all the wrong reasons if you don't. Clip and clean your fingernails, and brush dandruff off your collar and shoulders. Make sure your breath doesn't smell of coffee or other nose-pinching odours. Brush your teeth, or suck on a mint before the interview. Lastly, it goes without saying that you shouldn't chew gum during the interview.

Additional tips for women

A reputable company will only ever hire people based on the value they bring to the job and the business. With this in mind, it's advisable for women to be conservative in their dress when going for an interview. Wearing a short skirt or midriff-revealing top won't help you land a job. That latest creation from the fashion runway may look great, but make sure you can sit down comfortably while wearing it. Dress professionally in a skirt and blouse, and a jacket if this is relevant to the industry.

Your hair should be styled and off your face. If you wear it loose, make sure it's tidy and well groomed. Don't wear too much makeup or have painted talons for nails. Chances are you will have to use a keyboard as part of your job. Ensure your nails are manicured, and if you do use nail polish, choose a subdued colour.

Don't wear heels that raise your height to the level of a basketball player and make it difficult to walk. Medium heels and shoes that cover your feet are appropriate, and avoid sandals. Lastly, leave the flashy or ostentatious jewellery at home, keeping to smaller pieces only.

It's no mistake that there are more tips for men than women. In my experience, men are generally less concerned about their physical appearance than women, and over the last twenty-five years I have seen men make most of the above mistakes (with the exception of the dog collar).

I'm sometimes asked about tattoos. While there's no doubt that tattoos have become more socially acceptable in recent years, there are still negative connotations or personal biases attached to them. Most of those over forty may associate tattoos with motorbike gangs, the armed services, merchant navy or, even worse, a stretch in prison. Those who got tattoos as a younger person may be embarrassed by them in their mature years. Appropriate dress should succeed in covering them if this is a concern.

I knew a gentleman many years ago in his sixties who had had a rebellious youth, including time spent in jail. He had tattoos on his hands and fingers, and he went to the extent of having the tattoos surgically removed, which was a relatively long, painful and expensive process. While the suit he wore to church on Sunday covered the other tattoos, you would never have guessed his previous life as a career criminal.

Beyond the above tips, it's largely about using your own judgement.

CHAPTER 17

THE INTERVIEW #6 A TWO-WAY STREET

'Understanding is a two-way street.'
—Eleanor Roosevelt

After a good night's sleep, you'll want to ensure that you are well prepared physically and emotionally for the interview. If you've done your preparation, you should be a little nervous but in a good way; something called 'positive stress' will help you perform to your best during the interview. It's similar to an Olympic athlete lining up for the 100-metre sprint: after four years of training and lead-up competitions, they are ready to run the race of their lives, but they are still nervous, which helps them to focus.

What should you take with you to the interview? Back in the old days, when the interviewer-interviewee relationship was more geared towards a master-servant relationship, the meek and humble interviewee had a clear desk in front of them during the interview and the dominant, all-powerful interviewer had notepad, diary, pens and other associated paraphernalia. After the interview the candidate was sent home to await their judgement.

Fast-forward to the present and things are quite different. My strong advice is to treat the interview as a business meeting; a meeting in which you will also bring your notepad (or tablet computer), pens, paper and perhaps a copy of your resume. This should all be contained in a compendium or folder. You will have written out your questions ahead of time so you're prepared when the interviewer asks if you have any (although ideally you will have committed these to memory).

You should also make some brief notes during the interview to refer to afterwards. Clearly, you should not have your head down and be scribbling madly; instead you'll be catching key phrases or words that will prompt memories later of what was discussed.

Your impressions count too

As soon as you step into the office of the hiring organisation, you should be evaluating them as a potential employer. How does the receptionist greet you? Are they expecting you? Do they greet you by name? Offer you a drink? Do they ignore you? Do they keep talking to their friend on the telephone about their weekend while consciously ignoring you?

While none of these scenarios may be completely indicative of the organisation's culture, it's information you should be storing away for future reference if and when you get a job offer.

While sitting in reception, you can also pick up the vibe of the business by listening to voices and other noises coming from the office. Are there happy noises of enthusiastic conversations and laughter, or grey silence punctuated by the occasional phone ringing? Is the phone left unanswered? As people pass by, do they acknowledge you with a smile or do they walk past you with a sidelong glance? Take it all in, as it will form part of your consideration of the organisation and its culture as a potential employer.

There are many other things you can reflect on ahead of time. You have *passed the first hurdle*. You are at the interview because the organisation liked your resume. They see that you have the key ingredients for the job, as far as documented criteria are concerned, and they are interested in finding out more during the interview.

Remember that the interviewer or interviewers have themselves been interviewees at some time in their lives. They will know that you're feeling a little anxious and will give you some leeway for nerves. If you attend an interview and you don't feel this empathy—perhaps the interviewer dives right into tough, behavioural questions—you may rightly question whether or not you'd like to work for that person or organisation.

The interviewer wants you to succeed. When I was interviewing, I was always hoping that the person I was speaking to was *the one*. If I liked their resume I wanted to know more and, somewhat selfishly, wrap up the interview process this round and avoid having to repeat it at a later time, especially when I had a busy job with many competing priorities.

You have been invited to interview because you deserve to be there. The interviewer likes your resume, you have done the necessary preparation, and you're ready to give it your best shot. The interview is the penultimate stage of job search. You have made it through the initial cull of the application stage by having a great resume and now you have the opportunity to further spell out how and why you're a suitable candidate for the available role.

Now you also have the opportunity to ask the interviewer questions about the organisation and the role to decide if it's a good fit for you. As a result of the interview, both parties will have the information they need to make decisions.

After waiting in reception for ten or fifteen minutes you're approached by the interviewer with their hand outstretched in welcoming fashion. They introduce themselves and guide you to the interview room, which may be off reception or in the office itself. If it's in the office, you have an opportunity to get a sense of the company. You'll be able to check out the technology (do they have the latest PCs or stone tablets?), office decor, and the general vibrancy, or lack thereof, of the employees in the office.

Ask yourself if you can see yourself working there, with these people. While that could be construed as judgemental, it puts you on an even footing with the interviewer and the company considering you for employment.

You enter the interview room, and your interview journey begins.

CHAPTER 18

THE INTERVIEW #7
THE DAY ARRIVES

'Take time to deliberate, but when the time for
action has arrived, stop thinking and go in.'
—Napoleon Bonaparte

When you enter the interview room there will probably be a few moments of small talk with the interviewer, and with others as well if you're facing a panel. This is intended not only to relax you but also to allow the interviewers to get a general sense of you and your personality. This is important, because they will be deciding whether or not they could work with you, and how you would fit in with the rest of the team.

After the small talk, the interviewer (or the lead interviewer in a panel situation) will likely say something like, 'It's great to meet you, and thanks again for coming in today for the interview. We'll be interested in asking you about your background by reviewing elements of your resume, as well as asking you questions all the other candidates will receive. Before we do that, why don't you tell us a little about yourself?'

This question is the classic bridging question. We have moved from small talk and introductory formalities into the interview proper. The question itself seems rather harmless. Who can't tell an interviewer about themselves? For the unprepared, however, it can create an initial sense of unease as to how to answer it correctly given the breadth of the question.

In my experience, people tend to answer this question in one of two ways. They will start giving a potted history of their resume, which can often go on for several minutes if left unchecked, or they talk about their personal circumstances: 'I'm happily married and have two great kids and enjoy origami and waterskiing on the weekends.'

Neither of these responses is entirely appropriate, although the former is a better, albeit more long-winded, option than the latter.

A far better way of introducing yourself is to provide a concise, impactful and structured response that not only conveys the nub of who you are, but is completed in thirty to forty-five seconds. I suggest that you construct an introduction, or pitch, that has four elements and builds on your resume summary:

1. **Outline your vocation**: 'I am an experienced human resources business partner ...'

2. **Industries or companies you have worked for**: If you've moved around, don't include every one; just give the interviewer the flavour of the industries you've worked in:

'I've worked in transport and IT, most recently for …' or 'I've worked in diverse industries for companies such as …' If you've worked for a particularly well-known organisation, take the opportunity to mention it by name; people connect good people with good companies. If you mention Microsoft, Google or FedEx, organisations that people generally see in a favourable light, they will assume that you must also be good. Use this to your advantage. (Unfortunately, if you work for Joe Bloggs & Sons Transport Company, this may not work as well.)

3. **Key skills or areas of knowledge**: Provide three or four examples of skills or areas of knowledge you possess that relate to your vocation. An HR candidate could say, 'My key skills are in recruitment and selection, talent management and succession planning, and employee retention.' Don't be vague here; emphasise the best of the best skills you have, which will position you more effectively for the job you're applying for.

4. **Outline your strengths as an employee or manager**: Almost everyone in this situation lists strengths in communications, problem-solving, working as part of a team, stakeholder engagement, and a raft of other equally 'vanilla' talents. Why not differentiate yourself by teasing out the strengths unique to you? They will be more descriptive and more you, and you may elicit what I fondly call the eyebrow-raising response—in a good way.

The interviewer has probably heard all the usual old chestnuts many times over, so when you say something fresh and original they will take notice. Here is an example of a response guaranteed to get the interviewer's attention: 'My strengths include the ability to present complex IT jargon to a non-IT audience easily and effectively' or 'My strengths include developing effective and productive relationships with all levels of employees and managers within an organisation.'

Behind each of these wonderfully engineered strengths you will also have specific SAR stories to illustrate situations where you have demonstrated said strength. Don't fall into the trap of stating you have a particular skill or strength without being able to back it up with specifics. Instead, offer facts to support your assertion that you have used such skills and strengths successfully in previous roles and organisations. Be prepared to offer two or three examples to demonstrate how you've done this successfully.

Think of the above four steps as a billboard that paints the big picture of who you are professionally and forms a major part of your presentation in the interview. Make sure you have specific SAR stories for every achievement on your resume, as well as additional ones to demonstrate how well you match the essential requirements of the job.

What to expect during the interview

During the interview you'll also be asked typical clarification questions, and further behavioural questions. If you've done the necessary preparation you can probably predict (conservatively) around eighty percent of the questions you will be asked, or variants thereof. There is, however, questions you cannot predict.

Several years back I was interviewed for an HR manager's role. The interview was conducted professionally, and included initial small talk, an overview of what would be covered, and behavioural questions. At one point the local managing director asked me, 'If you had to invite three people to dinner, living or dead, who would they be and why?'

It would be impossible to prepare for a question like this unless you were a mindreader. I simply had to give it my best shot. Later, when I was offered the job, I learned that the MD asked all interviewees this question to see how quickly they could think on their feet. (I can't recall all the people I said I would invite, but one of them was my wife, with the explanation that I couldn't really leave her out. I think this impressed the MD, who was also a happily married family man.)

Try not to overcomplicate things regarding body language and risk ending up feeling self-conscious. If you're prepared for and excited about the interview, this will be reflected in your body language as quiet confidence and readiness. As Ralph Waldo Emerson said, 'When the eyes say one thing, and the tongue another, a practiced man relies on the language of the first.'

There have been many books devoted to the subject of body language so I'm not going to go over old ground. What I will do is present some basic information based on my own experience that I believe will serve you well in the interview room.

If you're prepared, you will be more relaxed. That doesn't mean comatose or reclining, but relaxed. When meeting the interviewer for the first time, a firm handshake, a smile and eye contact is essential for a good first impression. Yes, you may be a little nervous and the sweat glands on various parts of your anatomy may be working overtime, but the interviewer won't mind a bit of clamminess in your handshake. (If you sweat excessively, you could grip a tissue while you wait.)

As you take a seat, don't feel like you're strapped to an electric chair in anticipation of two thousand volts. Take a relaxed posture, with your feet on the ground and legs close together, or with your ankles crossed. Your arms can rest comfortably on the armrest or in your lap. Hand gestures are fine, but don't overuse them (or feel like your arms are attached with Velcro to the chair). A good interviewer will be doing their best to make you feel at ease. That way they can get the best from you.

It's also a good idea to rehearse the questions you might receive in an interview with someone you trust. This is beneficial not just in relation to the quality of information you convey when you answer the question, but it will also allow you to identify certain mannerisms and manage them appropriately. We're often not aware of our own mannerisms until someone points them out to us.

One person I worked with regularly, and irritatingly, thumped the table while answering questions. Another client liked to lovingly caress his earlobe as he thoughtfully responded to interview questions. As the interviewer, I quickly noticed these nervous tics, which only served to distract me from what the person was saying.

Wrapping up

Towards the end of the interview, the interviewer will ask if you have any questions (for which you are prepared) and once done with these, should outline the next steps in the selection process. If they don't volunteer this information, you need to ask what the next steps are. The interviewer will probably tell you they will contact you by a certain time or date.

Immediately after the interview, send a brief email to the interviewer or interviewers, thanking them for their time and, if appropriate, reaffirming your interest in the role. This is a small courtesy, but one that will be well received as so few candidates do it, probably only about five percent. If you are well thought of, it can speed things along and you may hear back sooner than you would have otherwise.

Receiving the verdict

Despite the best of intentions, many if not most organisations rarely contact interviewees when they say they will. If you are in transition, your sensitivities will be heightened. Your immediate reaction will probably be that they didn't like you and you've missed out on the job. Even though you know it's pure speculation, it will be a reflection of your state of mind.

Wait a few business days and, if you still haven't heard anything, follow up proactively with the interviewer. They might tell you that you were not successful. They might say that they've been too busy to respond to all the applicants yet. They might even tell you that you've made it through to the next round.

It's good to know where you stand, but even if you didn't get the job don't just accept the rejection and hang up. This is a great opportunity to ask for feedback, both in terms of how you didn't meet the requirements of the role, and your interview style.

Some companies will give you short shrift and provide very little or no feedback, perhaps fearing legal consequences, while others will be happy to give you constructive feedback. This feedback is particularly important as it means you will be even better prepared for your next interview.

— PART 3 —

MOVING FORWARD

— CHAPTER 19 —

POST-INTERVIEW REFERENCE CHECKS

'You will find it a very good practice to verify your references, sir.'
—Martin Routh, scholar

Put simply, reference checks are designed to provide interviewers with additional information about the candidate in order to make a hiring decision. Most references these days are obtained over the phone; however, it's not uncommon for organisations to conduct reference checks via email where the referee is interstate or overseas in a different, and inconvenient, time zone.

As a rule of thumb, the best referees are individuals you have worked with or known within the last five to eight years. Currency of information is critical in evaluating candidates.

Referees usually come from the following categories:

- Managers you have worked for
- Stakeholders within the business you have worked with or supported
- Employees who have worked for you
- Vendors, suppliers or customers outside the company you have had dealings with (especially if your job entails significant liaison with such groups)

It's very important to note that you should ask for your referees' permission to use them as referees at the *beginning* of your job search. You can lock them in later when you need their assistance for a specific reference check, but be sure to contact your referees before the recruiter or hiring organisation contacts them.

Once you have established that a referee will speak on your behalf, ask them to let you know when the reference check occurs. Given the opportunity to act as referees, some people like to string you along a little when providing feedback, but saying something like 'I told them what a ratbag you are and not to employ you in a million years' is not at all helpful. Once they are over channelling their inner comedian, hopefully they will give you a quick rundown on the questions asked, and any particular intelligence or feedback they gathered from the discussion.

While rare, during my early HR days I did have a couple of instances where the referee was surprised by my call and had not been approached by the candidate to act as a referee on their behalf. Needless to say, such oversights don't reflect well on the candidate and any inference can only be negative. When you do contact your referees, take the time to tell them about the role you have applied for. This will give them the context they need when the hiring organisation contacts them.

Helping your referee help you

Another important point is to ensure your referee shares some key information or points you would like them to convey. If the job you have applied for has a high requirement for effective stakeholder management, make sure your referee mentions this in the reference check and perhaps details a specific situation where you did well. There might not be a specific question on this topic, but there could be a catchall question at the end of the reference check asking if there is anything else they would like to mention about the applicant's suitability for the role.

If you have prepared your referee well, this will assure the hiring company that they have covered everything, they will volunteer further information that could be enough to get you across the line when it comes to comparing candidates and deciding who gets the job.

When organisations ask for referees, they don't usually specify who they would like to speak to, but will generally ask for someone you've worked for, which means that you can offer referees on your terms.

If you've worked for someone that you don't feel would represent your interests in applying for another job appropriately, don't put their name forward. Most people have experienced working for someone with a manager's title who may not provide a ringing endorsement of their professional background. You want to put forward someone who will speak highly of you in relation to the job you are applying for, and confirm that you're a good match for the required skills, knowledge and experience.

Common questions put to referees

Most organisations will ask for one to three referees and may specify the type of referee they are after based on the requirements of the job (internal stakeholder, manager). Upon contacting the referee, particularly by phone, the reference checker understands that most people are time poor and will only have ten or fifteen minutes in which to conduct the reference check. The purpose of the call is really just to examine the key aspects of the applicant's background.

Typical questions asked in reference checks:
- Can you confirm they worked with you on these dates in this position?
- How long have you known them?
- Why did they leave the organisation?
- How did they get along with other employees?
- Did they take excessive sick leave or other absences?
- Would you rehire them given the opportunity?
- Is there anything else about them we need to know to accurately evaluate them for the role?

Such reference checks are part of the protocol of interviews, and rarely, if ever, is a bad reference check received, but it's a tick in the box to validate what the interviewers have seen in an interview, and to provide more evidence for a hiring decision.

Occasionally, more often for senior roles, the informal network provides another key piece of information on individuals being considered for roles. While not a reference check per se, such informal information gathering can determine whether or not a job offer will be forthcoming.

While there are some vindictive individuals out there, most professionally-minded people will provide an objective evaluation of someone if asked. The advent and growth of LinkedIn also allows interviewers and recruiters to see how they may be connected to you and reach out accordingly. They could well reach out to these contacts informally if needed and particularly if there are any lingering doubts about an individual's suitability for a particular role.

Evaluating candidates after the interview

While I am personally not a big fan of over-egging the interview process with assessments, these are often used to further determine a candidate's suitability. Assessments fall into the following categories:
- Personality
- Ability, including abstract, verbal and numerical reasoning
- Aptitude
- Motivation/values
- Interest/belief inventories
- Integrity tests

If thorough interviews have been held and reference checks made, that should be sufficient information upon which to base a hiring decision.

The more information gathered, the more chance there is of something being raised that would constitute a worry or concern in relation to the final selection. Call it muddying the waters or something else, but I believe that organisations sometimes go too far in trying to get the perfect match in an area that is not an exact science.

Regardless, if you are asked to complete an assessment as part of the interview or selection process, you obviously need to comply. There is little chance to study for these beyond doing dummy tests on sites like www.shl.com, which will give you the opportunity to become more familiar with the tests and prepared to complete the real thing if asked.

Referees are an important part of the selection process, and used appropriately can give you a distinct advantage over other shortlisted candidates. Select the right people in the right roles to speak on your behalf and don't be afraid to coach them about what to say to the hiring organisation. Use every weapon at your disposal when it comes to getting hired.

CHAPTER 20

THE JOB OFFER

'I'm gonna make him an offer he can't refuse.
Okay? I want you to leave it all to me.'
—Don Corleone, *The Godfather*

You've finally made it through several interviews, reference checks and any other requirements the employer has thrown at you and are now waiting to hear back from the hiring company. This can be a frustrating time, especially on the back of a protracted interview phase. There are several things to keep in mind when you do receive the offer.

Understand what it includes. Ensure you understand all the components of the offer, not just the salary. Is superannuation included in the base or additional to it? This is an important point, because at the time of writing it can make a difference of 9.5 percent.

Benefits. In Australia, it's rare to include many other benefits on top of superannuation due to the fringe benefits tax (FBT) imposed on employers. Under FBT, employers pay additional tax on benefits beyond superannuation, particularly if they are not directly related to an individual's job, for example provision of a company car. There may be benefits like onsite parking, a laptop computer and a mobile phone, but these are all considered tools of trade; you need them to do your job effectively.

If you're moving into a senior-executive role, there may be more leeway for other elements of the offer, but for most people in professional or managerial roles the financial package offered is generally comprised of base salary, superannuation, and bonus or variable compensation.

Verbal offer. The first offer tends to be verbal; either the company, or the recruiter acting on their behalf will offer you the job over the phone. This should always be followed up by a written offer once the negotiations are finalised. During the delivery of the verbal offer, make sure you note down everything that's said so you can consider the total offer, not just to see if it meets your needs, but also to think about any questions you may have and perhaps put forward a counter-offer.

After receiving the offer. Once you receive the verbal offer, thank the person offering it, tell them you would like some time to consider it and respond with any questions, or your answer, as quickly as possible, certainly within twenty-four hours. This delay is not rude or offensive; it will give you time to review the offer and determine if you'd like to accept it as is, or would like to negotiate further.

If you feel pressured to give an answer about the offer then and there, don't succumb. Reinforce the message that you are grateful for the offer, but would like to mull it over before accepting. If there's continued pressure, you may start to think about whether this company's culture is what you're after.

Alternatively, there's no need to string things out if the offer made meets or exceeds your expectations. Accept the offer verbally and say you'll formally accept it once the written contract is received, at which time you will sign and return it.

Total package. Look at all the elements of the package—financial and non-financial—including base salary, superannuation, the location of the job, the person you will be working for, development opportunities available, and career paths.

If you look at the package this way, it will give you a clearer view of the offer and how it compares to what you were earning previously, or what you would like to be earning based on the market. Say, for example, you receive an offer that's $5,000 less on base salary than you would like, but instead of travelling forty-five minutes each way to work you will have an easy fifteen-minute drive against the traffic. How much is it worth to save this time? $5,000? $10,000? More? Different elements of the offer may be worth more or less to you based on who you are and what's important to you. While an easy commute would be attractive to many people, considerations like career development, training or leadership may be more attractive to younger workers.

I recently worked with a client who accepted a job for $10,000 less than what she was looking for principally on the basis that she would be working for a well-respected manager she had worked for a few years previously. She felt that the value of a good leader more than compensated for the drop in salary.

Negotiation. If you researched your salary options and shared your expectations during the interview, hopefully the offer is at or near this level. It's a personal thing, but you can either accept the offer as is, or negotiate further if you feel strongly that the salary is on the low side. Unless the employer tells you this is their final offer and it's non-negotiable—which should raise some concerns about their work culture—you can still negotiate; in many ways it's an expected part of the job-offer process.

Don't be greedy, but if you feel you're worth more, go back with a reasonable counter-offer. The worst they can say is no, and the best thing they can do is shell out a few more dollars to get you across the line; they will have a vested interest in you as their selected candidate.

Add some context to your counter-offer, rather than just asking for more. Maybe they are offering only a small increase over your last salary or package, or you're under consideration for another role that is paying more. Whatever the reason, I recommend stating this to give your counter-offer more weight and therefore consideration by the hiring organisation.

In situations where a job has been brokered by a recruiter, they will generally act as the go-between or mediator in salary negotiations. They have to strike a delicate balance; they don't want to appear to be pressuring the employer unnecessarily, but nor do they want to lose the selected candidate. As they are positioned between both parties, they can ensure that the negotiation process ends in a win–win outcome.

If the employer is limited by a certain budget and offers you less than what you would like, there's another strategy you can use to raise your salary: you can accept the remuneration as offered, but ask that there be another review of your salary in either three or six months, based on your performance against agreed metrics or objectives. Assuming you achieve your objectives, the organisation can then raise your salary accordingly.

This will work for them, as the salary budget three or six months after you start will generally be under the control of the hiring manager and less likely to be encumbered by too many other approvals. It's also a good investment on their part, because you will have made a quick and early difference during your tenure in those first few months.

These agreed targets should be included in the employment contract or offer letter.

Start date. Another aspect of the job offer and negotiation phase is the date that you'll commence working for your new employer. Employers are usually flexible, up to a certain point. Use your judgement and be attuned to any signals they may be giving off.

If you're presently unemployed, there may be nothing stopping you from starting work as soon as possible, perhaps within a few days. This could suit the hiring organisation, which would rather have people in place yesterday. Conversely, there's nothing to stop you from negotiating a start date in a week or two to allow you to enjoy some time without the stress of being between jobs. Believe me, there is a great difference here.

Planned holidays. Be sure to mention any booked or scheduled holidays early in the interview process, especially when the employer starts to make overtures about you joining them. It's best not to spring this sort of surprise on them when they offer you the job. It probably won't be well received if, after you thank them for the job, you inform them that you're leaving for Europe soon and won't be able to start for a month or so. In this case, the company would be within its rights to withdraw their offer.

You and the organisation want to start a working relationship without any concerns that could undermine it after a few months. Money issues can be insidious, so they are best dealt with up front during the negotiation phase. It's much more difficult to adjust salary once a new employee has started working in an organisation, so ensure that the package you receive is fair and reasonable based on the job you have been hired to do.

Once the negotiation phase is over and a package agreed on, the details will be documented in the letter of offer and employment contract, and sent to you via email or snail mail. Once received, sign the relevant documents and send a copy back to the employer. The offer is done and you're now ready to start your new job.

To reiterate, you should always know your worth in the market and what you're prepared to accept when offered a role. Use this information to negotiate a package that is appropriate and with which you are comfortable.

CHAPTER 21

STARTING YOUR NEW JOB

'The way to get started is to quit talking and begin doing.'
—Walt Disney

The alarm clock goes off earlier than it has during the preceding weeks or months. You extend an arm to hit the snooze button and then realise, with mixed emotions, that it's the first day of your new job. You're excited because it's what you've been working towards, but you feel some discomfort about being the new person. You're stepping into a new and different organisation, with a new boss, new colleagues, new team, new company systems, and new and different ways of doing things.

This is a great day, but also a day where you need to be aware of the things you should be doing and not doing in the coming weeks and months to ensure all the hard work that got you here won't go to waste.

Think about the impression you want to make upon joining your new employer. This is also in the context of the probationary period you are covered by. During this time the organisation, and more particularly your manager, will determine whether you're worthy to keep on permanently after observing your performance and contribution over the first three or six months of your employment.

There are a number of things to keep in mind as you start your new job.

Arrival. Get to work at the specified time, which could be a little later than the regular starting time to allow the hiring manager to ensure everything is in place for your arrival. In most cases they will have an orientation or induction schedule for you for the coming days. Hopefully, the new organisation or manager will be expecting you. I say hopefully because I've worked in organisations where the new employee arrived at reception only to be told that the manager was away travelling and had clearly forgotten about the new hire starting that day.

First meeting. In an ideal world, your new manager will greet you when you arrive, following which you might have a debriefing meeting in their office over a cup of coffee. This could also be when you're issued with a staff ID badge, asked to sign some paperwork, and briefed on administrative issues relevant to new employees.

Tour and introductions. Once you have been briefed by your new manager, they will likely take you on a tour of the work area, during which time they will introduce you to various people, show you where the bathrooms are, where to get a coffee, and how to use the security ID.

As you meet people, be sure to give them a firm handshake, look them in the eye and try to remember their name (almost impossible, I know, but do your best).

Generally in these situations, your boss will introduce you by name and title, plus explain where you have worked previously. There will follow a little small talk, generally of the welcome-to-the team variety, and you will then move on.

Settling in. Once the tour is concluded, which should take thirty minutes or less, you'll be taken back to your workstation or office and encouraged to settle in. Your boss might say they will check in with you again at lunchtime, and in the meantime you will be assigned another colleague to be your buddy or go-to person as you open the drawers on your desk and check out all the nice new stationery that's been purchased for you.

Now that you're in the office and settled in your ergonomic chair that requires a PhD in physics to operate, you have the opportunity to ponder everything you need to do over the coming days and weeks. Here are some suggestions that will help to ensure success in your new organisation.

Interaction with your new boss. When you meet with your boss in the early days, try to obtain all the information you can about what's important to them. Find out what their expectations are. This may have been raised during the interview process, but it's worth revisiting. Important information would include their key objectives, and any frustrations they are experiencing that you could address.

Regular meetings. Schedule regular meetings with your new boss to ensure complete alignment in the early days of your tenure, particularly in relation to priorities and key work assignments.

Organisational charts. Ask for a copy of all relevant organisational charts as soon as you can. This will allow you to see at a glance how the organisation is structured, but more importantly, whom you need to meet with as you settle into your new role. This could include colleagues all reporting to the same manager as well as internal clients or stakeholders that you will be supporting. For example, if you're an HR business partner you will want to meet with all the members of the executive team you'll be working with.

Map of the office and contact details. Finding your way to the bathroom and getting back to your desk after going to the photocopier will be much easier in the early days if you have a map of the office layout. Likewise, contact details of all interstate or overseas staff will be invaluable.

Meet your colleagues. This includes internal clients. Schedule face-to-face meetings in the first week or two, if you can. This is not only a chance to meet your peers and other stakeholders, but also to dig deeper into their specific organisational needs and how you can help address them.

If you have staff reporting to you, it's a chance to get to know them and understand what they are working on. For interstate or international colleagues, a phone call or Skype session may be more effective. Plan for these meetings by documenting a few questions or issues you would like to explore.

See if you can get hold of relevant organisational charts, business plans or presentations that may be useful in getting you up to speed sooner rather than later. As you know from the interview process, first impressions are very important and you want to leave each of these first meetings with a trail of good first impressions as a foundation for the future.

Look for early wins. Building on the initial meetings, a good way of ensuring early credibility is to produce, solve or develop something that makes an immediate difference to those you have met. You might obtain this information during your meetings with your internal clients, or maybe you came across it during the interview when you asked why the previous incumbent left the job.

For example, you may note that in speaking with your staff that your predecessor ran infrequent and poorly managed meetings. Based on this, you can quickly schedule and develop an impressive agenda for the first team meeting. It's all about actions rather than hollow promises and talk.

Understand the communication culture. How does your manager communicate? What communication do they prefer, face-to-face, email or phone? This knowledge will serve you well as you communicate with them. More broadly, is email used within the organisation more often than phone calls or office visits? How do people write emails? What tone is used? What organisational norms are in place? If you're unsure, ask.

Additionally, become familiar with the jargon and acronyms of the business. If a term is used during a meeting that you don't understand, ask someone what it is and what it means. Make notes and ask after the meeting. Being able to speak the language of the business sooner rather than later is an important ingredient to success.

Spend time with the IT person. You will likely be faced with a myriad of new systems, applications and software in your new organisation. On that basis, try and get some time with the IT person and relevant others so you're familiar with all the organisational technology as soon as you can. Technology is prevalent in most organisations and forms the basis of a lot of company operations. The sooner you're familiar with the jargon the better off you'll be. Oh, and the IT person can let you know how to switch on your new laptop.

Check in with the boss regularly. I suggest twice-weekly meetings over the first month and then weekly by the second month. This will be a very positive move as it ensures that the two of you are in synch, and it provides ongoing access to someone who should be able to answer most of your questions as they come up. Regular check-ins will also give your boss firsthand updates on what you're working on, and how quickly you're getting into a rhythm in your new role.

Ask for feedback on things you have started working on, even if it's feedback you may not want to hear. It's better to hear it early on, act on it and improve what you can rather than find out during the end-of-probation discussion, when it may be too late and place you in jeopardy.

Take notes. Buy a notebook, or use your tablet or laptop, and keep notes of all your conversations and associated actions. This will force you to be organised, keep commitments and achieve objectives you have either set for yourself or received from others.

In the early days your boss and other stakeholders will undoubtedly send a lot of information your way. By taking notes, you will be able to prioritise, and even discuss, recommended courses of action in a timely manner.

When starting a new job, you will generally have a honeymoon phase of a couple of months where you are the new person and there's some forgiveness or leeway if you don't always know things and have to ask lots of questions. You need to be in sponge mode from day one and not only absorb the information but retain it as best you can while looking for early wins to reinforce the organisation's decision to hire you.

— CHAPTER 22 —

TIPS FROM HUMAN RESOURCES PROFESSIONALS

'Human resources isn't a thing we do. It's the thing that runs our business.'
—Steve Wynn, business magnate

During your job search journey, you'll undoubtedly have some interaction with human resources professionals with varying labels: director, manager, people and culture manager, talent acquisition specialist, or any number of other grandly titled individuals within the HR world.

Unless you are an HR professional looking for work in an HR team, most often the HR folks you meet will be acting as gatekeepers and influencers in the hiring process. Their responsibility could be to manage the entire selection process, or they might play a minor role only, depending on the organisation's culture. In recent years there has been a trend for HR to step away from direct involvement in the hiring processes. At the same time, hiring managers have been handed increased autonomy and subsequent accountability for hiring.

Your first discussion or meeting with an organisation could be with an HR person who will conduct a screening interview over the phone and also participate in interview panels. Whatever role they take, HR personnel are part of the recruitment and selection process so it's important to get their perspective on what constitutes success in job search.

For this book, I interviewed several senior HR professionals and have compiled a list of questions and responses that I hope will prove helpful to mature jobseekers.

As an HR professional, what do you look for in potential candidates?

Cultural fit was the main response here, and this relates largely to what is important for the organisation. It could be customer-service attitude, the ability to learn, or exceptional communication skills. Each skill is then investigated as part of the recruitment process via interviews and assessments.

What are the most common mistakes made by the over-forties in job search?

Overwhelmingly, HR experts maintained that focusing on age is the most detrimental aspect to job search for the over 40s. They all agreed that age is immaterial; in most cases potential employers won't care about age unless you yourself care about age.

Resumes prepared by the over-forties are often too long and sometimes look dated. Older jobseekers should refresh their resumes to ensure they are contemporary and resonate in the current job market. Resumes should be adapted for the role being applied for and key selling points should be strongly conveyed.

How do hiring organisations generally view the over-forties?

Excluding their own organisations, the HR professionals raised several points in relation to this question. There is a mindset among some organisations and hiring managers that the over-forties are slower to learn, more difficult to manage, and sometimes mired in traditional management styles. These individuals might not be as strong on the latest technology, but this is something that could be countered by ensuring they have a strong LinkedIn profile, and a fresh, contemporary resume.

What value do the over-forties offer to organisations?

In a word, experience. Older people have vast life experience they can draw on to make better decisions, and more effectively deal with different types of people and circumstances. This experience relates to both successes and previous learning opportunities.

Do the over-forties have opportunities to succeed in the hiring process?

HR professionals claim to not even think about age; they say they just look for the best person for the job. The key criterion is whether or not the person has a solid and diverse resume indicating they have the required skills and experience. Furthermore, when managers are trained in effective hiring practices this benefits older workers since the managers are focused on hiring the best person for their job. Ultimately, success in being offered a position happens irrespective of age.

What can the over-forties do specifically to ensure a positive outcome in job search?

It's always a good idea to be open and honest about any gaps in employment history, the reasons for leaving the last job, redundancy, or any caring responsibilities. Also, it is of particular value to employers if jobseekers demonstrate knowledge of current issues, markets, and trends in their particular industry or profession. Be proactive with networking, even while employed. Those who are employed should keep in touch with their external network of contacts outside their current organisation.

What is a common way for organisations to source candidates?

Understandably, this varied by organisation, but otherwise there were no real surprises. Some companies focused predominantly on internal networks and referrals, with the occasional online advertisement. The use of internal networks allowed potential employees to be pre-screened on organisational values by existing employees (who, it's fair to say, have some skin in the game to ensure the referred employee succeeds).

Some organisations do not use agencies, preferring to advertise directly online with SEEK or Adzuna, two of the dominant online job boards. One organisation did not have a paid referral program, but still found that existing employees, who were clearly engaged, introduced friends, relatives and acquaintances for roles. Other organisations offer a cash incentive for successful referrals ($2,000 was the amount quoted).

What does a typical selection process look like?

Most HR professionals use a similar hiring process, but each has their own way of filtering candidates in order to make a final selection.

These methods include phone screening, or an initial interview with an internal HR or external recruitment professional; assessments, behavioural or competency-based interviews; case studies; reference checks; decision to hire; and finally a job offer.

Can older candidates affect younger hiring managers?

Younger managers can sometimes be intimidated by older jobseekers and prefer to hire younger employees. This is true in some organisations, while others make a point of training new managers to focus on hiring the best person for the job. This may come back to unconscious bias, but it's important for the older candidate not to appear as a threat, or worse, arrogant. Most of the time, the more mature employee is seen as a safe pair of hands and an attractive prospect.

What general advice can you offer older jobseekers?

The advice was wide-ranging and insightful. Resumes should stand out from the crowd. They should be well written and concise, and address the key selection criteria of the job applied for. Tired-looking resumes usually go straight into the *maybe* or *no* piles. With all candidates, dress and appearance is important.

During the interview, all candidates should be prepared with behavioural examples to demonstrate specific skills. Many candidates across the board don't prepare for this, and understandably perform poorly during the interview.

Finally, older jobseekers should let go of any fixation with age; they shouldn't justify their age, and neither should they overcompensate for it. Age is an issue only for those who allow it to be.

So there you have it, some insight and practical advice from HR professionals, who very often have stewardship over hiring practices in their organisations. The key takeaway is that age is a state of mind and is really only an issue if you let it be.

CONCLUSION

My goal in writing this book is to share experiences and knowledge with you, and to be your companion during job search so you don't have to go through it alone. It's a rare person that can succeed with any venture in isolation. Even the very best executives and CEOs have coaches to provide support and guidance.

I have no doubt that you will benefit from what I've presented in this book. It can be a lot to digest if you haven't been out of work or in job search mode for several years, but it's about taking steps in order to give yourself every chance of landing that ideal next role, whatever it may be. If you do everything outlined in this book thoroughly and diligently, the information will help you obtain your next role by differentiating you from other candidates and giving you a distinct advantage every step of the way, from determining the sort of work you do to receiving a job offer.

By this point you should be clear about the role or roles that interest you, and how they match up with your values, skills and interests. You are now savvy enough to research the market in which those roles can be found, and to get out into the market via a networking strategy.

You have developed a resume that is effective in selling your skills and experience, and which will enable you to get to more interviews and subsequent job offers.

You have developed an online presence by establishing and populating a LinkedIn profile. You're confidently using a number of online job boards such as SEEK and Apply Direct, and are receiving daily emails listing vacant jobs that suit your background and match your aspirations.

You have been introduced to or found recruiters who genuinely want to understand who you are and what you offer. These recruiters will put you forward for roles with the right employers.

You understand the dynamics of preparing for, conducting and following up on an interview. You have also heard from a number of HR professionals and recruiters about what they look for in candidates.

You can reach out to referees and ensure that they represent you appropriately. You know what to be aware of to make your transition into your new role a successful one.

Clearly, getting a new job is very different from the good old days. It does require effort and often means you might step into new and not completely familiar domains, which may include the online world.

As someone who is over forty, I hope you have come to understand that age is not a barrier in job search unless you let it be. As we've seen, most recruiters believe that age is immaterial in the selection process and is very often an advantage, given that mature workers can bring to the table experience, wherewithal, knowledge, stability, maturity and good judgement.

If your job search is taking longer than you would like, don't give up; stick at it. Continue to review your job search strategy to ensure that you're doing everything required to land your next role. This will include participating in the visible job market of recruiters and online sources, but predominantly should include getting out there and engaging with people, building relationships and networking. Historically this is where most jobs are found and should be where you expend most of your job search effort.

A recent *Forbes* article[4] found that most jobs are not advertised; these unadvertised jobs are otherwise known as the 'hidden job market', and it is estimated that this sector accounts for up to eighty percent of hires. This number has been debated, but the numbers are still high enough that if you're not networking, you're not accessing roles.

I wish you all the best and a long, successful and happy career in whatever you choose to do.

---

4 '6 ways to crack the hidden job market', Nancy Collamer, *Forbes, 12 August 2013*, www. forbes.com.

AN INTERVIEW WITH SEEK

The following is based on an interview with Joe Powell, managing director of SEEK Education:

With over seventeen years' experience connecting candidates to job opportunities, and organisations to candidates, SEEK remains the leading online employment marketplace in Australia. The site receives around thirty million visits per month, but more importantly it delivers 22 percent of placements in the Australian market, which equates to approximately 660,000 people every year going into a new role they found on SEEK.

'We invest a lot of resource into delivering the best search and matching experience to both candidates and hirers,' Powell says, 'and it's through this that we're able to deliver more placements than any other online job site. Placements are the real measure of value provided to the market, so it's a position we're very proud of and continue to build on.'

For many people, SEEK is synonymous with job search because it invests in their brand, and the name 'SEEK' equates to jobs. SEEK also offers aligned services such as education and training to support job moves and career development (SEEK Learning), volunteering opportunities (SEEK Volunteer), and self-employment (businesses for sale in SEEK Commercial).

Powell says that the way people think about their careers has changed. There is an understanding now that a career can take many paths, and education and volunteering can play an important role in this. The way candidates and hirers connect has also evolved. 'Previously hirers would simply post a job advertisement and wait for applications,' he says, 'but now we're able to marry really sophisticated data analytics against our five million SEEK profiles to offer real-time connections between hirers and candidates.'

Through their SEEK profiles, jobseekers are now able to receive recommendations for roles they can apply for immediately via their mobile device. Similarly, hirers can receive recommendations for highly relevant candidates that match the roles they are trying to fill.

SEEK covers a broad section of the employment market, which can be seen from the following compensation levels for advertised jobs:

Roles less than $50K	12% of roles advertised on SEEK
$50–$100K	57%
$100–$150K	24%
$150–$200K	4%
Over $200K	3%

While the majority of roles on SEEK are in the $50–$100K range, nearly one-third have annual compensation over $100K. Powell believes SEEK will see increasing numbers of senior roles being advertised (over $200K) as confidence in the market increases and companies start to hire at this level.

For many people aged over forty, the emergence of different technologies and social media can be overwhelming. Believing that such technology and strategies are only for younger people, they may be reluctant to try an unfamiliar approach. To overcome this, SEEK employs a whole team of user-experience staff whose sole purpose is to ensure that SEEK is a simple, and intuitive, tool to use.

SEEK also provides other types of support. For example, on the home page users can select 'Contact us' and view a range of frequently asked questions, and contact SEEK by sending a message, making a call, going through social-media platforms such as Facebook or Twitter, or using the SEEK chat room. 'SEEK is agnostic about how we interact with users [to the site],' Powell says, 'but we facilitate how the client wants to interact.'

Beyond using SEEK for job search, jobseekers can also set up a SEEK profile within the system. This involves filling in the fields with your career history, skills and qualifications, and role preferences, as well as attaching a copy of your resume. Once you have fully completed and activated your profile, potential employers searching for suitable candidates based on their own requirements will be able to find you.

Powell reports that currently there are around five million profiles on SEEK and this number is growing. Over the course of the year ended June 2014, there had been around 280,000 interactions with profiles on SEEK, meaning that employers are searching for suitable candidates within SEEK itself. Given the future growth in this area,

Powell strongly advises jobseekers to establish and maintain a complete profile on SEEK in order to be found by employers.

Just as social media continues to grow in popularity, the way in which users interact with SEEK is also changing. The biggest shift in technology is the increased use of mobile devices such as phones and tablets to access information online. For SEEK, mobile-led access to the site accounts for about sixty percent of visits.

This on-the-go access will increase, according to Powell. As a result, SEEK will continue to deliver what their clients want by providing more mobile access and functionality, including but not limited to users' ability to edit their SEEK profile on mobile devices. 'We're focused on delivering a seamless experience for SEEK users, regardless of how they access the site,' Powell says.

Powell believes that in the future communication via video will be an important and ultimately standard part of job applications, technology that SEEK will support. In this scenario, applicants will submit an application for a role, which will be *viewed* rather than read, and the applicant will be scrutinised and screened directly by the employer.

When asked for some specific tips for jobseekers over forty who want to stand out in job search, Powell offered the following:

- If you're applying for jobs online answer screening questions with clarity, detail and honesty.
- Have a 'spot-on' resume that conveys exactly who you are and how you meet the requirements of the job you have applied for.
- Have a level of passion for what you want to do because enthusiasm counts for a lot in job search.
- Understand the organisation you are applying for and ensure you are aligned with them on things like values, vision and culture.

ABOUT THE AUTHOR

Paul Di Michiel (the Career Medic) has an honours degree in psychology and over twenty-five years' corporate experience in senior human resources roles in IT, transport and logistics, and manufacturing with such iconic organisations as Federal Express and Orange Business Services.

In addition to his extensive professional experience in the Australian market, Paul has also worked in Singapore and the United Kingdom in senior regional and global human resources roles. In recent years, Paul moved into the career-transition arena and has achieved great success for his clients, as well as gaining personal satisfaction in making a difference. Nothing gives Paul more joy than to see a client successfully move into a new and exciting role.

Paul has experienced job loss and job search himself on several occasions and can empathise completely with his clients. His aim is to take the worry out of job search and demonstrate how finding new employment can be approached in a practical, confident and ultimately successful way.

Paul and his wife Leearne live in Sydney, Australia and have four children, Elise, Edward, Isabella and James. Paul enjoys photography, particularly action photography, and has a penchant for anything involving horses.

To learn more about Paul, or receive updates and information on topics related to job search, visit:

Website	www.thecareermedic.com
Blog	http://thecareermedic.com/blog
LinkedIn	https://www.linkedin.com/company/the-career-medic
Facebook	https://www.facebook.com/thecareermedic
Twitter	https://twitter.com/TheCareerMedic

particularly action photography, and has a penchant for anything involving horses.

To learn more about Paul, or receive updates and information on topics related to job search, visit:

Website	www.thecareermedic.com
Blog	http://thecareermedic.com/blog
LinkedIn	https://www.linkedin.com/company/the-career-medic
Facebook	https://www.facebook.com/thecareermedic
Twitter	https://twitter.com/TheCareerMedic

www.ingramcontent.com/pod-product-compliance
Lightning Source LLC
Chambersburg PA
CBHW070719220326
41598CB00024BA/3234